Genuine Christianity

Millennial Mind Publishing
An imprint of American Book Publishing
5442 So. 900 East, #146
Salt Lake City, UT 84117-7204

www.american-book.com
Printed in the United States of America on acid-free paper.

Genuine Christianity

Designed by Jana Rade, design@american-book.com

Publisher's Note: American Book Publishing relies on the author's integrity of research and attribution; each statement has not been investigated to determine if it has been accurately made. The author and publisher specifically disclaim any responsibility for any liability, loss, or risk, personal or otherwise, which is incurred as a consequence, directly or indirectly, of the use and application of any of the contents of this book. In such situations where medical, legal, or other professional services may apply, please seek the advice of such professionals directly.

ISBN-10: 1-58982-483-0

ISBN-13: 978-1-58982-483-6

Library of Congress Cataloging-in-Publication Data

Low, L. F.
Genuine Christianity / L.F. Low.
p. cm.
Includes bibliographical references and index.
ISBN-13: 978-1-58982-483-6
ISBN-10: 1-58982-483-0
1. Christian life. I. Title.
BV4501.3.L69 2009
248.4--dc22

2008040579

Special Sales: These books are available at special discounts for bulk purchases. Special editions, including personalized covers, excerpts of existing books, and corporate imprints, can be created in large quantities for special needs. For more information e-mail info@american-book.com.

Genuine Christianity

L. F. Low

Dedication

This book is dedicated:

To my Teacher, the Holy Spirit, without whom, there would be no Genuine Christianity in actuality or in book form. You taught me all I know and led me to do this work. Thank you for the excitement of just knowing you. Knowing the Holy Spirit is experiencing Jesus and that is the greatest pleasure and treasure of all.

To the love of my life for over forty-five years, Dixie my wife and constant companion for the past forty-three years, without whom I wouldn't have made it far in life at all. Thank you dear Dixie, for your constant support and encouragement has kept me pushing on in pursuit of being genuine as a husband, man of God and friend. You have always been there for me and for that, I will be eternally thankful. You are a gift to me from Jesus Himself.

Foreword

I have been working with churches and ministries for many years. During this time, I have observed people get born again and drag all kinds of emotional baggage with them into their walk with the Lord and ultimately for some, their positions in leadership. They would succeed in suppressing their past emotional scars for a season, but never properly dealt with, those hurts, bruises, addictions, and the like, would surface in time and tragically destroy relationships, families, jobs, churches, and ministries.

Larry and Dixie Low have received an awesome word from God on how to let the love of Jesus deal with these issues, and enable individuals to walk in the true freedom that our Lord Jesus purchased with His shed blood.

Genuine Christianity is a book that covers every aspect of the Christian life. It is easy to read, easy to understand, and easy to apply to one's daily life. I believe it is a must read and will benefit every believer on all spiritual levels. The book definitely points the reader to Jesus for help, not man.

Thank you, Larry and Dixie, for obeying the Lord by fulfilling the ministry that He has called you into. Your obedience has resulted in countless people being set free, enabling them to be more effectual as they walk and work together with the Lord Jesus Christ and finish the course that the Lord has set before them.

Dr. Jim Kaseman
Founder and President of AFCM
Association of Faith Churches and Ministers Intl.

Why Read This Book

Good question. That's the question I always ask myself when someone hands me a new book or I hear that some book is a 'must read.' In order to help me settle that question in your mind however, I must ask a few questions and verbally paint a few scenarios that will help identify *Genuine Christianity's* audience. If by chance, you do not find yourself as a member of this audience I want you to know that reading *Genuine Christianity* will equip and empower you to *minister*[1] life to those who

---

[1] As Christians, we are all ministers of restoration and reconciliation to those within our scope of influence. Proof is in Galatians 6:1-2, 2Corinthians 5:18-19 and John 14:12. We are not all called into an office of leadership within our

are in this audience. I believe the church is suffering a critical shortage of those who are equipped and willing to help others.

The Questions

Have you ever wondered where emotional pain comes from or why we humans hurt emotionally? Have you ever wondered why, after being born again, we are still dealing with emotional pain? Have you ever felt like everyone else in the church seems to have it all together but you? Have you ever said, "I don't want to be some phony hypocrite like So-in-so!" yet all the while feeling like you are just like "So-in-so"? Maybe you are one who is becoming very tired of playing the, "I'm blessed brother" game while feeling like there is a huge curse over your life keeping you from receiving God's best.

Maybe you are a frustrated pastor who feels like some of the people in your church are there to make your life miserable. Or, maybe you still believe that the cause of a Christian's misbehavior is their sin or a lack of desire to really follow the Lord. After all, you have told them how to live, you have tried your best to set an example and you pray for them daily; what

---

local church. However, we are to live as Jesus lived (1John 2:6) by interacting with our culture as a source of healing and freedom for the oppressed masses.

more could you do and what else could be making them cause such trouble? Or, maybe it is a struggle living what you preach; is the stress of faking it till you make it about to get you down?

You may be one who is getting very tired of hiding your secret. You know, if you ever let the cat out of the bag, your life in that church will be over; maybe even in your community. Maybe you are being tempted to give up; after all, it seems to be getting harder all the time to be a Christian. Have you ever wondered why walking in love is so hard? Did you know it is possible to live in perfect inner peace with no fear or any kind of inner turmoil? In fact, did you know that inner turmoil and fear can actually help you toward becoming *genuine*?

Do you believe that your past should stay in the past and should no longer have power over you? However, your past will not stay in the past and you wonder what is wrong with you because it feels like the past is happening repeatedly each day. Would you like to know why your past keeps bugging you? Would you like to know how to deal with your past that keeps pestering you?

Maybe you are just tired of wearing your mask and working so hard to make everyone believe you are happily operating in the joy of the Lord. Tired of feeling irrelevant, worthless, all alone, dirty, trapped, shameful, inadequate, unworthy, and angry? Maybe you are tired of hearing, "Just get over it!", or you may feel like your feelings don't count. Many feel like they are all alone in the middle of a crowd and no one hears them or seems to care. Fed up with taking all the pills because they only numb you and have not given you back your life? Or maybe you are tired of feeling as if a black cloud hangs over your life.

If any of this spoke to you, *Genuine Christianity* will help you identify the cause of your feelings. It will also identify the things that are holding you back in your walk with God by teaching you how to receive the permanent freedom for which you have been searching and deserve. The goal of this book is to define what being *genuine* as a Christian means and then to help you uncover how simple it is to live a life of *genuine Christianity.* Therefore, let's begin our journey.

Table of Contents

Introduction.. 1
The Genuine Christian Understands and Practices Proper Communication 13
The Genuine Christian Is Born-Again 19
Genuine Christians Understand the Power and Importance of the Printed Word of God.. 27
A Genuine Christian Portrays a Living Hope 35
A Genuine Christian Has Developed Genuine Faith 47
A Genuine Christian Relies on God to Renew His or Her Mind 53
The Genuine Christian Lives a Life of Rest and Peace...................... 67
The Genuine Christian Lives a Holy Life 79
The Genuine Christian Understands the Love Walk.......................... 95
A Genuine Christian Gives Up the Ways of the Flesh.......................109
Controlling the Thoughts of the Mind 113
Exercising Your Authority..123
Genuine Christians Properly Deal with Their Anger.........................131
Forgiveness from the Heart..141
A Genuine Christian Fits into the House of God...............................145
The Genuine Christian Understands We Were Chosen to Praise God 157
Genuine Christians Are Submissive to Authorities............................165
The Genuine Christians Live a Higher Standard 173
The Genuine Christian as an Employee..183

The Genuine Christian's Physical Health 187
The Genuine Christian's Relationships 193
Genuine Christians Live to Bless Others 199
Genuine Christians Serve and Receive from One Another 217
Genuine Christians Live a Life of Humility 225
Freedom Means You Are Free to Choose 239
Appendix i 245
Appendix ii 253
Appendix iii 261
Appendix iv 265
Appendix v 283
Bibliography 285
General Index 287
About the Author 297

Introduction

> **Genuine** \ 'jen-je-wen \ adj [L *genuinus* native, genuine; akin to L *gigner* to beget more at KIN] 1 a: "Having the reputed or apparent qualities or character actually produced by or proceeding from the alleged source or author. Free from hypocrisy or pretense: SINCERE syn see AUTHENTIC gen-u-ine-ly *adv* gen-u-ine-ness (Webster's New Collegiate Dictionary – Fourth edition)

This phrase of *genuine Christianity* has captivated me for over twenty-five years. Where did this phrase come from and why is it so captivating for me? It came from the mission and vision the Lord gave me many years ago. If you have read anything about finding the vision and mission for your life, you already know that your vision is not something you create or find — no, it finds you. The encounter with my vision and mission occurred directly following my career change from computer analyst to minister of the Gospel. Let me share with you the mission statement my wife and I received.

Our mission in life is: "To call people out of spiritual apathy and into a higher walk with God through a committed lifestyle of *genuine Christianity*."

The vision, of course, spells out the details of how to accomplish the mission, but for now, this book will discuss the mission or journey of becoming a "*genuine* Christian."

Now for the question of *why* this phrase captivates me. The word *genuine* paints a very different picture of Christians than what I typically see in the Christian community today. Genuine is something or someone who is *real,* not phony, made up, put on, or hiding something. Someone who is genuine is faithful, consistent, honest, and responsible. Becoming genuine produces a quality within the Christian that makes him able to respond to the needs of others. This ability to respond makes Christians relevant and needed in the world today.

In becoming *genuine,* we set ourselves apart, with the help of the Holy Spirit, to be totally obedient to Jesus' written word and to the Holy Spirit's spoken word. For too many years now, many have looked for ways to receive more blessings without giving much thought to the need of becoming more obedient. The 'bless me' motivation is wrong and is changing because it is shallow and self-serving. I believe the majority of the church is tired of the shallowness of self-serving religion and are looking for ways to become blessings to others rather than receive blessings. It is my firm belief that we can make a difference in this world, but not without some change involving sacrifice and personal discipline. Jesus said it this way; *"If anyone desires to come after Me, let him deny himself, and take up his cross, and follow Me"* (Matthew 16:24). I believe the time is now. I believe the majority of the church is ready to become the men and women of God that will be blessings to the multitudes. That will happen as they learn how to allow the Holy Spirit (our teacher) to lead and teach. Jesus said we *cannot* do it on our own (John 15:5) so we must learn what it means to abide IN Christ. Just because the Holy Spirit is alive in you is no sign you are abiding IN Jesus Christ. Learning how to be obedient to Jesus through the Holy Spirit is abiding in Him or becoming *genuine.*

Genuine Christians are as capable of responding to the cry of their culture as Jesus was to the culture of His time. *Genuine* Christians do not fit into the world's view of things. They are willing and *able* to react in a positive way to the cries of those trapped by today's culture. They respond not in judgment, but in a way that brings freedom to those suffering with pain created by today's fast paced, self-centered world. In order to help those who are crying out for freedom we must be as free of the affects of our culture as Jesus was from the culture of His time. A *genuine* Christian not only has the right message but also knows how to produce the fruit of Jesus Christ — the fruit worthy of repentance (Matthew 3:8). A *genuine* Christian is truly a spiritual stranger traveling through a land of multi-religions with physically and emotionally damaging cultural customs and rituals.

A non-genuine Christian is one who fits into the cultural customs and rituals without even thinking about it and does not understand how damaging and unsafe the culture is. The non-genuine Christian who sees the resulting damage and the emotional pain can only wag their finger or shake their head in disgust while proclaiming some judgmental statement about those who are responding from their pain. Unfortunately, there are many, calling themselves Christians, who do not even see the damage or the danger within their culture. These, I believe, are the ones addressed by the Apostle Paul when he said, *"Awake, you who sleep, Arise from the dead, and Christ will give you light. See then that you walk circumspectly, not as fools but as wise, re-*

deeming the time, because the days are evil. Therefore do not be unwise, but understand what the will of the Lord is" (Ephesians 5:14-17).

Well, what is the will of the Lord? The book of Romans teaches that we will only find the will of the Lord as we work to renew our minds (Romans 12:2). Working with the Lord to renew your mind is waking up, arising from a dead, non-productive religion to a life of light, power, and new abilities to redeem the time, not only for yourself but also for others needing your help. *Genuine* Christians are awake and alert with a good understanding of God's will for their own life while helping redeem the time for others who are crying out for help. *Genuine* Christians are confident in their ability to help others find the freedoms they themselves are enjoying.

I know the body of Christ will benefit greatly when ministers quit telling people what they ought to do and begin to show them *how* to do it. For years, I preached on the *problem* and the *promise* without ever mentioning the *process* needed to erase the problem and obtain the promise. I didn't mention it because I did not know how to show them the way. When I learned how, my ministry took on a completely new dimension that produces change in people's lives *instantly*. Now I mention the problem, teach on the promise, and minister the process. As the Christian community benefits from our increased abilities, so will the non-believing world. In fact, Romans teaches us that very point, *"For the earnest expectation of the creation eagerly waits for the revealing of the sons of God"* (Romans 8:19). Those in the world are eagerly waiting for you and me to come into our own as God's children. To come into our own is a graduation from childhood to sons proving our maturity as Christians. Mature Christians, or sons, are able to *respond* to the needs of others without concern for their own life's issues.

Unfortunately, the Christian community has more *preachers*

than *ministers* and that must change if the Body of Christ is to ever enjoy freedom from their inner pain and fears. You may be thinking, 'What's the difference between preachers and ministers?' A *preacher* will tell you that because of Jesus' work you should already be free, hoping you get hold of it. A *minister* leads you to the Healer, helping you apply the healing balm staying with you until you have it. A *preacher* appeals to your intellect while a *minister* touches your heart and soul. We desperately need the *preachers.* However, we need *preachers* who know how to produce *ministers* as directed in Ephesians 4:12, "*for the equipping of the saints for the work of ministry, for the edifying of the body of Christ.*"

There are many good programs out there proving that the Christian community recognizes it needs help. However, the programs that I am familiar with fail in the same common area; they do not set up the meeting between the hurting and the Healer. They tell you what is wrong, they tell you the possibilities and many of them tell you what needs to be done but we need one more step. We need people who are confident enough in their relationship with the Healer, to help the hurting by facilitating the meetings as well as the communication with the Healer. There is more to our Christian faith and ministry than telling people how to live. We are, or should be, equipped to *show* them by our life's testimony. We must begin to fully use our faith in the spiritual power (Acts 1:8) Christ invested in us, in order to become free from our inner pain and fears. This is *working out our own salvation with fear and trembling* spoken of in Philippians 2:12. For this action is proof that it is God who is at work within us causing us to desire, as well as to accomplish, His perfect will and His good pleasure (Philippians 2:13).

Just what does it take to become a *genuine* Christian? Do you know? I hope you do! However, in this era of committing to something or someone only until it gets difficult or inconvenient, too many believe it is not possible or necessary to attain that level of commitment in our faith today. I firmly believe this level of commitment is possible to attain once we deal with our fears and inner feelings. As long as we continue to run from our fears and inner feelings, pretending they do not exist, we continue to delay the long desired *great harvest* and the second coming of our Lord.

Some may wonder how the church can delay the great harvest. I will tell you. The delay of the great harvest is occurring because we are unable to take care of the hurting masses, since the church contains as much inner pain as does the world.

We cannot help people get free if we ourselves are in bondage and willing to live with our pain. Unless the people outside the church begin to witness people inside the church living with peace and freedoms they cannot obtain on their own, they will not come. And why should they come if they cannot find the help they are seeking?

Our life is to be a continual witness of the redemptive power of Christ for all who believe. Until Christian's lives begin to exhibit our redemption and freedom during everyday life, it doesn't matter what our message is because the non-believers have no reason to pay attention. In other words, if you cannot reconcile your own relationships, how are you going to help those who are outside of Christ? If you cannot live in this world free from inner turmoil and fear, how are you going to help those outside of the church find peace?

As long as church leaders continue to divorce their spouses, spiritually and emotionally abuse their congregations and live compromised, hypocritical lives, how can we expect the non-believing world to pay attention to the greatest news ever given to mankind? Until we, the Body of Christ, begin to produce the fruit of Christ in our daily lives on a mass scale, the hurting non-believers will continue to ignore our Good News. Our lives speak louder than our message. This, I believe, is delaying the latter day's great harvest and final outpouring we have all longed to see. It is time to make whatever changes are necessary to become *genuine* Christians.

This belief and passion of mine is my primary purpose for writing *Genuine Christianity*. It is also burning within me to alert the church that, in many ways, I believe, we are missing the beauty and the power of God in our daily lives by complicating what God intended to be simple, peaceful and restful. If that is true, then that may explain why we see local churches struggling to prove their relevance and struggling to stay alive. If we can see it, we can fix it and get about doing the works of Jesus.

Therefore, if you sense a need to become more *genuine* at any point in this journey, then join me by allowing the Holy Spirit to transform your life. If, by chance, I am only rehearsing what you already know, then won't you join me in praying for the maturing and healing of the Body of Christ on earth today? The world, our culture, desperately needs the healing power of the church and the hour is late. When the trumpet of God sounds, we must be found doing the Works of Jesus (John 14:12), not licking our wounds pretending it doesn't hurt, playing the religious game. The world does not need any more religion. You will not be religious if you aim your sights on becoming a *genuine* Christian. Remember, Webster says being genuine is, *"Having the reputed or apparent qualities or character actually produced by or proceeding from the alleged source or author."*

To start with, there are two things on which we must all agree; 1) Jesus is the author and finisher of our faith (Hebrews 12:2) and 2) Jesus was not, nor is He, a "religious" person. He, in fact, came to earth to replace the need for religion by making it possible for mankind to have a relationship with God. In Matthew 22:37-40, Jesus teaches us that the greatest commandments are *to love the Lord with all your heart, mind and soul and to love your neighbors as yourself.* Jesus goes on to say that, all the Law and the Prophets hang on these two commands. In other words, everything God has ever done, for or with mankind, from the beginning through this very moment, hangs or rests upon the foundational scriptures of loving or relating to God and our neighbors. In John 13:34-35, Jesus taught that we would be identifiable as His disciples when we *love others* as He loved us. There it is — our challenge! We cannot meet that challenge by being religious. Jesus didn't and neither can we. Our success or failure as Christians hang on our ability to "relate" to our Father in heaven and to each other as Jesus related to His Father and His disciples. That demands a "mature, spiritual" connection, not a "religious" one. In order to be effective and accomplish the works Jesus has laid out for us, we must improve our ability and, in some cases, our desire to build and maintain better relationships on this earth.

Relationships with one another are horizontal while our relationship with God is vertical. When these relationship types come together in life, as they should, they form a cross, the central symbol of Christianity today. I pray that the cross will be a constant reminder of the need and our responsibility to relate horizontally with one another, as well as vertically with God. As we see in the next few pages, you cannot have one without the other.

That being said, I think if we take a good hard look at the Body of Christ we can see a major problem staring back at us — our ability to relate to each other and the inability to love (agape) as Jesus has called us to in John 13:34-35. Much of the

Body struggles with consistently being *loving* toward one another when God has called us to *be* a channel of His love. Many are working hard to live in line with 1Corinthians 13:1-8 without first, fully understanding how to abide in Him. God has called us to abide in Him (1John 3:24) and to walk like Him (1John 2:6), which then automatically lines us up with 1Corinthians 13. This sets us free from a lifestyle of self-defeating works. Marriages within the Body are struggling with an increasing number failing each year. Even our personal relationships within the church, much of the time, are unhealthy, resembling TV soap operas more than a unified body. This mentality causes people to fight for position and control, create alliances, and keep record of wrongs done by others. A healthy church works as one body for common goals, with the ultimate goal of reflecting God's glory. Due to improperly dealing with the inner pain and struggles all humans deal with, manipulation of one another occurs, creating *strife in relationships within the church*. We cannot love each other while jockeying for position and hiding behind masks of protection. It is impossible to reflect God's glory this way! I do not believe people desire this condition to be their experience; they just do not know how to change it. *Genuine Christianity* will teach you how to change it.

Could it be that we are making life far too complex? Could it be that man's insane desire for religion has unknowingly caused our relationship with God to become a complicated series of works once again? I think so, and that quest for simplicity, as well as the ability to be *genuine* as a Christian, responding to the needs of others, has driven me for the past quarter of a century. It is in my mind every time I read the Scriptures. It drives my study time efforts and it motivates my preaching, teaching and the pastoral counsel I offer others. This is where the "rubber of Christianity" meets the "road of experience" with its challenges, twists, and turns faced by all.

My desire is to help you see how to reverse this condition and to experience, in your personal life, what many are already experiencing in their life and in their church. I am not going to share some untried and untested philosophy with you but something that has worked successfully with many common, ordinary people for over two thousand years now.

We are not talking about principles to help you live a better life or some self-help process; we are talking about literally walking with God. We are talking about abiding in Christ (John 15:7) and being hidden under the shadow of the Almighty (Psalm 91:1). We are talking about becoming *genuine* Christians.

We are called to follow Jesus and when He announced He was beginning His ministry He said, "The Spirit of the Lord God is upon me, because the Lord has anointed Me to preach good tidings to the poor; He has sent Me to heal the broken-hearted, To proclaim liberty to the captives ... " (Isaiah 61:1). We are called to minister the same way (John 20:21). We have learned well how to deliver the Good News and now it is time to learn how to minister healing to the brokenhearted. That will begin to happen as soon as the body begins to live it in their personal lives.

We will begin in the Book of 1Peter, chapter one. We will refer to and cross-reference many other Scriptures as well, but 1Peter will be our basic guide through this adventure. The Holy Spirit through the Apostle Peter not only teaches us what a *genuine* Christian looks like and acts like, but, most importantly; it is the *How to* of becoming *genuine.*

There are many attributes mentioned in the book of 1Peter that will identify you as a *genuine* Christian. More than identifying every attribute Peter mentions, my goal is to help identify stumbling blocks you may encounter and to help you see their origin and the simplicity of eliminating them as you journey toward becoming *genuine*. There will be some of 1Peter we do not touch or mention, but I hope this trip we are taking together opens your eyes to attributes and understandings of our faith that may have, to this point in your walk, potentially gone unnoticed. My prayer is that you see the *relationship revelation*, contained in 1Peter, which will cause your spiritual growth in the attributes mentioned. Likewise, I also pray that by applying and consistently living by the attributes and principles I do mention, this will help you acquire the attributes I do not mention.

In the Apostle Peter's opening statement, he introduces himself, identifies his credentials, identifies his audience, and then most importantly, spells out with wonderful clarity his goal for writing this letter and what we can expect to gain by following the instructions the Holy Spirit lead him to write. For quicker understanding, I will quote from the Amplified version of the Holy Bible for the first two verses of 1Peter.

"Peter, An apostle (a special messenger) of Jesus Christ, [writing] to the elect exiles of the dispersion scattered (sowed) abroad in Pontus, Galatia, Cappadocia, Asia, and Bithynia, Who were chosen and foreknown by God the Father and consecrated (sanctified, made holy) by the Spirit to be obedient to Jesus Christ (the Messiah) and to be sprinkled with [His] blood; May grace (spiritual blessing) and peace be given you in increasing abundance [that spiritual peace to be realized in and through Christ, freedom from fears, agitating passions, and moral conflicts]" (1Peter 1:1-2 Amplified).

There are two main points that must be highlighted here in order to understand Peter's intentions, as well as our goal for writing and reading this book; 1) We were chosen and foreknown by God the Father and consecrated by the Holy Spirit for the purpose of *becoming obedient to Jesus Christ.* 2) We will gain an inner peace and a confidence in God that will bring us *freedom from fears, agitating passions and moral conflicts* that, unfortunately, most are currently running from.

> I, for one, am tired of running and ready to get on with it. I am ready to become all I can be for and through Jesus Christ. Will you join me? I do not want my loved ones or yours subjected to the moral, physical, and mental decay of this world any longer and I believe God is calling us to put an end to it. That end will come when we get serious about becoming *genuine* and follow Jesus in faithful obedience by learning to hear and follow the voice of the Holy Spirit. That end will come when we begin to relate to God the way Jesus taught us by honestly communicating with Him about *everything.*

The Genuine Christian Understands and Practices Proper Communication

"So then, my beloved brethren, let every man be swift to hear, slow to speak ... For we all stumble in many things. If anyone does not stumble in word, he is a perfect man, able also to bridle the whole body" (James 1:19; 3:2)

What is the foundational material of every relationship? Another way of asking that would be; what must we humans do in order to have a relationship? If your answer was "to talk," you would have been one third correct. If your answer was "to communicate," you would have been correct. However, it is important to understand entirely what communication means and the parts that make up the whole of proper communication.

All communication begins with talking. We must have something to say and a desire to say it before any type of relationship, horizontal or vertical, can begin to grow. Many people have deep and wonderful thoughts and feelings, but if not expressed, they will never have a relationship. A relationship is born when someone has a desire to "relate" or share his or her life and his or her experiences with someone else. All relationships are born out of need. For instance, a young man has a strange loneliness that drives him to hunt for just the right young woman to take as a bride. The young woman seeks protection, love, and desires to build a family so she begins to look for the man of her dreams. A sick person seeks a doctor while a teacher seeks those willing to learn and the spiritually empty searches for one who is confident and spiritually satisfied. All the challenges of life drive us toward others in the hope of finding help to make life easier, more meaningful and fulfilling.

This creates another challenge: The people that problems drive us toward can become additional problems if we do not understand the remaining two parts of communication. Why? Because it takes *effective* communication to start a relationship and without effective, complete communication, there is nothing to feed the relationship. A relationship is like any other living thing, *if you do not feed it*, it will die. This includes our relationship with God as well as with people. How we relate to others on the earth is the same way we will generally relate to God.

Part two is listening. If we only talk without listening, we do not have a relationship. When we never take time to listen during a conversation, we are rude and classified as having a social disorder. To listen indicates that you expect others to have something of value to say to you. To listen says, "What you have to say is important to me." If what they have to say is important, then it stands to reason that the one saying it must also be important. Meeting the emotional needs of all parties occur during the simple process of speaking and proper listening. This feeds and grooms our relationships.

In order to build and strengthen relationships, listening requires more than the physical use of the ear. In fact, those who have no physical capacity to hear sound relate much better than many who have perfect hearing. This is because the hearing impaired must practice *active listening*. This is not only hearing, but also *observing* the one speaking. In other words, we must look at, or direct our attention toward, those who are speaking to us. Effective communication is concentrating on, not only the words communicated but also on the one communicating.

That same listening skill works as we build our vertical relationship with God. Of course, we cannot physically see God, but we must direct our attention toward Him by learning to be still on the inside. When God speaks, it comes as a *gentle knowing* on the inside; it is knowledge or an understanding that is not a product of your thinking process.

To hear from God you must cease your thinking temporarily. This is generally a problem for those who have an overactive mind. They must learn to control their mind so their mind does not control them (2Corinthians 10:5). If you do not quiet your mind, you will miss many blessings from God because you will not receive or hear what He is saying. I have known many who said God does not speak to them. As we began to help these individuals, it didn't take long before they began to understand that God always speaks, but they had never quieted their mind enough to receive it.

So far we have "*speaking*" + "*listening*". The third part that many do not understand, especially when relating to God, is "*responding*". If you ask a question or make a comment that the person you are communicating with responds to, there are times when a response is required of you to complete the communication. Many times, it is only a courteous "thank you," but there will come a time when it will be important to ask another question. If, while communicating, I receive a reply that I don't understand, I will ask another question, make another statement, or even give another example. I have dealt with those who hear the response and go away confused rather than get a clearer understanding. This is especially true when it relates to communicating with God. If He says something that requires another question, then ask Him the question.

In every failed relationship, we can be sure that communication broke down before the relationship ended; but, *what makes communication break down?* The answer to this is so simple you may reject it at first. The thing that makes communication break down in all the relationships we have dealt with is simply, *bad feelings.*

Somehow, we have learned, in error, to ignore and run from our bad feelings. This is a common error because generally we have failed to understand what those bad feelings are telling us. Therefore, we do not know what to do with them. Bad feelings can benefit you, as I will soon explain.

We believe that if others say or do something that result in our feeling bad, then the other person is the cause of those bad feelings. In most cases, that simply is not true. The truth is that words and actions from others merely activate bad feelings already stored in our memory from some previous experience. Discovering this simple but powerful truth increases our ability to communicate by reducing the threat caused by our emotional pain.

Our communication formula is, therefore:

Talking + Active Listening + Responding = Communication

Any part of this formula left out destroys communication, horizontally as well as vertically. After a while, when there is a lack of listening or responding, the desire to continue the relationship dies, leading to the relationship's end. When we attempt to communicate with God, but fail to receive a response from Him or fail to respond to Him ourselves, we may give up and settle for the thought that maybe He only talks to the pastors. Nothing could be further from the truth. Communication takes time. It takes effort. It takes a true desire to "relate" to the one with whom we are communicating. This formula and its simple concepts for effective communication with humans (horizontal communication) apply as well when building a relationship with God (vertical communication).

Many people *think* about God much of the time. However, how much actual communication takes place? How much verbal communication do you do with God? Does He know the sound of your voice because you are always calling on Him? Jeremiah 33:3 says, *"Call to me, and I will answer you, and show you great and mighty things which you do not know."* The first three words are, "*call to me*" not "*think to me*" or "*think about me,*" but "*call to me.*"

Equally important, do you know the sound of His voice? Is your faith in Him developed to the point that you believe He desires to speak to you about the detail issues of your life and therefore, you always wait, quietly for His reply? Too many people speak to God on the run and rarely give Him a chance to reply to them. Or, if they do receive a reply, they rarely do anything with it in the way of "responding" to Him or speaking out what He has said. This is the foundation for maturing as a *Genuine* Christian. On this foundation, we will build an in-depth understanding of what being *genuine* as a Christian is all about. But first, some of you may be wondering what it takes to become a Christian in the first place.

There was a time in my life when I erroneously believed I must be a Christian just because I wasn't born a Jew or a Muslim. I have talked to others who believed that Christianity is just another religion or ideology that can help those who are weak and unable to succeed on their own. If you have this book in your lap, you are obviously looking for some truth that makes sense so let's begin at the beginning. How does one become a Christian?

The Genuine Christian is Born-Again

"…having been born again, not of corruptible seed but incorruptible, through the word of God which lives and abides forever" (1Peter 1:23)

A *genuine* Christian knows they are born again through the Word of God. The term "born-again" is not a 20th century term. It is a term coined by Jesus and reported in the Holy Bible in John 3 when He was conversing with Nicodemus about spiritual matters. *"Most assuredly, I say to you, unless one is born again, he cannot see the kingdom of God …. Most assuredly, I say to you, unless one is born of water and the Spirit, he cannot enter the kingdom of God. That which is born of flesh is flesh, and that which is born of the Spirit is spirit. Do not marvel that I said to you, that you must be born again"* (John 3:3, 5-7). To be *born of water* is referring to the natural birth process of the flesh. God's law stipulates that one must live in a body of flesh, bone, and blood to be capable of affecting anything on this earth. That is why spirits of fallen angels (demons) strive with mankind to possess their bodies.

The same law applies to God and that is why it is so important for the Christian community to understand the need to become *genuine* in our faith and our relationship with God. To be *born-again* is relating to our spirit being reborn by, the Holy Spirit infusing with our spirit as we invite Jesus to take over our lives. Simply going to church does not make you a Christian. Tithing and doing good works does not make you a Christian. You can only hope to be *genuine* as a Christian if you have become a Christian at all. If you have never asked Jesus to take over your life then you are not born-again. If you are not born-again, you are not a Christian.

The 20th century phrase *born-again Christian* is an oxymoron. You cannot be a Christian unless you are born again. There is no other way of becoming a Christian. Becoming a Christian is becoming "Christ like" in the very core of our nature. Our spirit needs to be resurrected from the dead, due to the sinful nature of mankind, which occurred when Adam chose to sin in the Garden of Eden. Until we are born-again, our sinful nature is controlling us. Therefore, our spirit without God is powerless. During the born-again experience, our spirit comes alive with Christ Jesus by an infusion with, or an incarnation of the Holy Spirit. Our sin nature is also made non-effective, during this experience by *a circumcision not made with human hands* (Romans 6:6, Colossians 2:11) and we become the *righteousness of God in Christ Jesus* (2Corinthians 5:21). This is the born-again experience. Without it, you are not a Christian.

If you are not certain that you are born-again, then you probably are not. Romans 8:16 says, *"The Spirit Himself bears witness with our spirit that we are children of God."* In other words, we know that we know when we are born-again. The Holy Spirit who comes to dwell within us confirms that we are born-again.

"Most assuredly, I say to you, unless one is born again, he cannot see the kingdom of God." (Jesus Christ - John 3:3)

Being born again is a decision each person must make for him or her self. Being born again is a decision we each must reach on our own. All humanity faces the understanding that something is missing in life and then must decide what, if anything, they desire to do about it. Every human spirit is yearning to be reconnected to its creator — God. Every human spirit knows the feeling or will experience the disconnected feeling from something very important and fundamentally basic for happiness and security. That something is really *someone*. It is, of course, God. Every person will one day experience a basic weakness and insecurity about life that will also drive him or her to investigate the possibility of there being a God. God has put within all of us an understanding that one day we all must give an account of how we spent or invested our life (2Corinthians 5:10). All of these feelings and experiences are designed by God to draw us to Him, for we were, after all, created for His pleasure (Colossians 1:16 & Ephesians 2:10).

God loves every human being ever created. No one was a mistake in God's eyes. Your parents may have referred to you as a surprise or a mistake, but you were neither one to God. The Bible says, *"For you formed my inward parts; you covered me in my mother's womb … My frame was not hidden from you, When I was made in secret, and skillfully wrought in the lowest parts of the earth. Your eyes saw my substance, being yet unformed. And in Your book they all were written, the days fashioned for me, when as yet there were none of them"* (Psalm 139:13, 15, 16).

God has a detailed, life-long plan for every human. In Jeremiah 29:11, He teaches us, "For I know the thoughts that I think toward you says the Lord, thoughts of peace and not of evil, to give you a future and a hope." You may think your life is a waste, but there is no such thing as a wasted or useless life in God's eyes. He has a plan for you. He also knew exactly what you would have to go through before you and He met. From the moment of your conception in your mother's womb, He has been waiting for you and drawing you to Him.

He loves you very much. Your works will not earn you a place in His family (Ephesians 2:8-9, Titus 3:4-6). You need only ask Him to take you just as you are. You don't have to clean yourself up or learn anything at all; all you have to do is to want Him and understand that you really don't have much of a chance in life without Him. (John 15:5). If that is where you currently are, then the rest is easy. Just ask Him to be your Lord. Our salvation comes by His grace; it is a gift from God to you. *"For God so loved the world that He gave His only begotten Son, that whoever believes in Him should not perish but have eternal life"* (John 3:16, emphasis added).

When you speak to God, talk to Him from your heart. In other words, mean what you say but speak it from your mouth (Romans 10:10). I know of many people who said a prayer just because someone asked them to but they didn't really mean it therefore, it was a waste of their time. God knows our motivations better than we do. God knows when we are serious and when we are just trying to look good to others (1Samuel 16:7). When you do talk to Him about your eternal life, speak audibly to Him. Tell Him you need Him and that you believe that Jesus died for your sins. When you understand that Jesus paid for the forgiveness of all your sins and that God the Father raised Him from the dead so that our faith in Him would be justified, you then merely invite Jesus into your life and into your heart. If you were to invite me into your home you would just say, "Welcome, please come in and make yourself at home." Well, that's the attitude and all you do when asking

God to make you a part of His family. What about confessing your sin, some may be wondering. When you see your life and the trail of destructive sins of your own doing, you will understand your need for a Savior. When you come to that realization, you will also naturally feel remorse for those things in your life and you will therefore ask God to forgive you. You couldn't remember all your individual sins if you tried. All God wants is one with a repentant heart (Psalm 51:17). A repentant heart means you are ready to turn and start out in a new direction. If you have to tell someone to say they are sorry for their life's decisions, then they are not ready to be born again. Well, I hope that you decide to join God's family if you haven't already. Remember, just a simple request, inviting the Lord into your life and into your heart is sufficient. He is a gentleman and will not push His way into your life.

Connecting to a good church is important to help you grow in the things of God. Ask God to direct you to a church that preaches and teaches the Word of God. As you read and study this book, you will also see many things that will happen as you grow in the things of God and learn how to walk after the Spirit of God. You need a good pastor who will pray for you, encourage and counsel you as you grow and develop. Now that you are part of the family of God, you will naturally desire to serve God somewhere. The church is the structure through which we serve others, which is serving God. Look at Ephesians 2:8-10, *"For by grace you have been saved through faith, and that not of yourselves; it is a gift of God, not of works, lest anyone should boast. For we are His workmanship, created in Christ Jesus for good works, which God prepared beforehand that we should walk in them."*

Remember, God Himself has planned our life in detail. Knowing that makes it our adventure to find the path, He has prepared us to follow. He has some very exciting things for you to discover and to experience!

If, by chance, you are still exploring the possibility of becoming a Christian, I invite you to look in the back of this book for my personal congratulations and my invitation to dialogue with you concerning your newfound faith or your questions and concerns about Christianity in general. I wish to help you any way I can. It will be more helpful for you to first finish reading *Genuine Christianity* because of the many questions you may have. If by chance, I do not address them to your understanding or satisfaction, I will welcome them and respond to them as quickly as I possibly can.

Knowing that you are born again you must also understand that now you are more than just a mortal human being. I hear Christians use the excuse that they made wrong choices or failed at something because they are human. "What do you expect — I'm only human!" they say. Well that just is not true after you are born again. Let me quote 1Peter 1:23 from the Phillips Translation for you.

"For you are not just mortals now but sons of God; the live, permanent Word of the living God has given you his own indestructible heredity."

You and I are spirit people indwelt by God Himself. We have access to all the wisdom of heaven (James 1:5). We have been given the Mind of Christ (1Corinthians 2:16) if we will just draw upon it. We have divine protection (Psalm 91). We have a personal Helper, Counselor and Teacher (John 14:16, 26). We have the authority of Christ Jesus Himself (Luke 10:19) and we have been given use of Jesus' Name (Colossians 3:17). And one more thing, if all that is not enough, we have been seated in heavenly places far above God's and our enemies (Ephesians 2:6, John 14:20). We can no longer use the excuse that we are only human.

Being born again does not make us better than the unsaved but it does make us forgiven of all our sin, spiritually clean and free of a guilty conscience (Hebrews 9:14) with a much greater chance to live in His peace (John 14:27), rest (Hebrews 4), joy (Romans 14:17) and hope (1Peter 1:3, Romans 5:1-5). In other words, for a *genuine* Christian, living life in Jesus Christ makes life, make sense.

I feel the need to mention one more thing along these lines that I think is very important. *Genuine* Christians love to lead others to the Savior and help them grow in the things of the Lord.

The book of wisdom says, *"The fruit of the righteous is a tree of life, and he who wins souls is wise."* (Proverbs 11:30) G*enuine* Christians become trees of life. Their life becomes attractive enough to the troubled world that the world will begin to seek you out for help, for wisdom, and for encouragement. In fact, *genuine* Christians are always ready to give an answer to those who ask what gives them such hope (1Peter 3:15).

G*enuine* Christians are those who no longer hide their light (Matthew 5:14-16), but instead, allow it to shine to all around them. They are the ones who win the souls of those who come and, believe me, they do come.

In Daniel 12:3 we see, "Those who are wise shall shine like the brightness of the firmament, and those who turn many to righteousness like the stars forever and ever." Do you want to shine as the earth shines? There is no other planet in the entire universe that shines like the earth. You can shine like the earth by becoming real — genuine, by turning many toward Christ. For eternity, they that win souls shall shine like the stars in the heavens forever and ever! Hallelujah!

If winning souls sets off fear in you, then you need to tell the Lord. He will help you prepare for the adventure of your life. Do not think that the fear will go away on it's own as you learn more about the Lord. If you do not address it specifically and allow the Lord to deal with it, it will stay with you.

I have known many who have been in the Lord for many, many years and have never won anyone to the Lord. They seem to fall prey to the fear of not knowing enough. If you know that Jesus loves you, saved you, and desires all mankind to receive salvation, you know enough. Talk to the Lord about your fear and He will chase it off. *"There is no fear in love; but perfect love* (Jesus) *casts out fear, because fear involves torment. But he who fears has not been made perfect* (mature) *in love"* (1John 4:18, comments added).

The Lord will deal with your fear if you allow Him. When you have the faith to tell Him what you are afraid of, you are inviting Him into your situation. This invitation frees God to deal with the situation that is keeping you in bondage to fear. If you do not tell Him about your fear, you are not inviting Him to help you. God can only move on our behalf when we invite Him. He will never push His way into your life. He respects your freedom to choose and has promised to never take away your free will.

I want you to shine like the brightest stars forever, and the only way to conquer fear is to talk to the Lord about it. If you don't whip fear here, it will run you around forever. I would rather see you shine forever. Wouldn't you? *Genuine* Christians allow Jesus to whip their fears rather than allowing their fears to whip them.

Genuine Christians Understand The Power and Importance of the Printed Word of God

"...having been born again, not of corruptible seed but incorruptible, through the word of God which lives and abides forever" (1Peter 1:23)

There is one thing essential to getting born again — the printed Word of God. Everything starts from a seed. The Word of God is the incorruptible seed (Mark 4:14) that produces faith or trust in God. Without trusting God or understanding God's ways, how could anyone be expected to trust Him for their eternal life, or anything else for that matter. Listening to or reading the Word of God, plants this incorruptible seed in your heart. This provides us with the understanding necessary to make the decision to even consider becoming a Christian. The Word of God is the information and inspiration that draws us closer to God for building a *relationship* with Him. One who has a relationship with God, based upon their faith in what Jesus did for them, is a Christian.

I think it is very important to mention therefore, that *genuine* Christians need only one foundational source of printed inspiration for their faith. That source is the scriptures found in the Holy Bible, made up of thirty-nine books of the Old Testament and twenty-seven books of the New Testament. *Genuine* Christians believe that *"All scripture is given by inspiration of God, and is profitable for doctrine, for reproof, for correction, for instruction in righteousness that the man of God may be complete, thoroughly equipped for every good work"* (2Timothy 3:16-17). We also believe *"that no prophecy of Scripture is of any private interpretation, for prophecy never came by the will of man, but holy men of God spoke as they were moved by the Holy Spirit"* (2Peter 1:20, 21).

Because of this fundamental belief, the Holy Bible containing the sixty-six books from Genesis through Revelation is the Gospel to the *genuine* Christian. We need no other foundation. There are many wonderful books written to help explain the ways of God. I hope you consider this book one of them. However, in order for any of them to be helpful and spiritually healthy for the reader, they must always lead you back to the Holy Bible. The Holy Bible must support them or else the knowledge gained may very well be spiritually unhealthy. God has given mankind one book with which to govern his life, it is the Holy Bible – the *Word of God.* Other proofs to us are the experiences gained from simply reading the Word of God contained within these sixty-six books. Even more proofs occur when you begin to apply the information contained within the Bible as well.

"I am not ashamed of the gospel of Christ, for it is the power of God to salvation for everyone who believes, for the Jew first and also for the Greek. (Non-Jew)" (Romans 1:16, explanations added).

No other book can make this claim because it cannot deliver on a promise like that. However, applying the words of the Holy Bible will change your life and your eternity.

The message contained within these sixty-six books brings Jesus Christ into full view. No other book does that.

> *"Nor is there salvation in any other, for there is no other name under heaven given among men by which we must be saved."* (Acts 4:12) *"Jesus said to him, 'I am the way, the truth, and the life. No one comes to the Father except through Me.'"* (John 14:6)

This message of Jesus sets men free from the power of sin and brings life into focus. No other book does that. Other religious books bring men under the control of men who are usually deceased and unable to save themselves. He who cannot save himself cannot save others. Jesus, on the other hand, was dead but is now alive. No other man has ever done that.

The words contained within the Holy Bible feeds you. You are spirit and your spirit needs feeding just like your physical body. You feed your physical body physical food but you, the spirit man need spiritual food (John 6:63). A genuine growth takes place within our spirit when we read and meditate on the words contained within this volume of sixty-six books. No other book does that.

> *"As newborn babes, desire the pure milk of the word that you may grow thereby."* (1Peter 2:2)

> *"I fed you with milk and not with solid food; for until now you were not able to receive it, and even now you are still not able; for you are still carnal. For where there are envy, strife, and divisions among you, are you not carnal and be-*

> *having like mere men?"* (1Corinthians 3:2, 3)

The Bible teaches, as well as experience verifies that immaturity is the result of not reading and applying the Word of God.

> *"For though by this time you ought to be teachers, you need someone to teach you again the first principles of the oracles of God; and you have come to need milk and not solid food. For everyone who partakes only of milk is unskilled in the word of righteousness, for he is a babe. But solid food belongs to those who are of full age, that is, those who <u>by reason of use</u> have their senses exercised to discern both good and evil."* (Hebrews 5:12-14 emphasis added)

Out of sheer curiosity, I have read some other religion's bibles or books of discipline, and though many contain interesting philosophies, none of them fed and strengthened my inner man like the Holy Bible. None of them led me to the source of salvation, Jesus the Christ.

> *"Beware lest anyone cheat you through philosophy and empty deceit, according to the tradition of men, according to the basic principles of the world, and not according to Christ."* (Colossians 2:8)

Genuine Christians regularly feed their spirit by reading the Holy Bible — the Word of God.

The Word of God warns us of man's continued attempts to overthrow God's plan.

> *"But there were also false prophets among the people, even*

> *as there will be false teachers among you, who will secretly bring in destructive heresies, even denying the Lord who bought them, and bring on themselves swift destruction. And many will follow their destructive ways, because of whom the way of truth will be blasphemed. By covetousness they will exploit you with deceptive words; for a long time their judgment has not been idle, and their destruction does not slumber."* (2 Peter 2:1-3, emphases added)

The very last word of these sixty-six books, called the Holy Bible, foretells the coming problem and delivers the sternest warning of all. *"For I testify to everyone who hears the words of the prophecy of this book; If anyone adds to these things, God will add to him the plagues that are written in this book; and if anyone takes away from the words of the book of this prophecy, God shall take away his part from the Book of Life, from the holy city, and from the things which are written in this book. He who testifies to these things says, 'Surely I am coming quickly.' Amen. Even so, come, Lord Jesus! The grace of our Lord Jesus Christ be with you all. Amen"* (Revelation 22:18-21).

When the Holy Spirit speaks to you, He will never lead you outside the confines of the Holy Bible. There is safety when you know where the fences are. The Holy Spirit will always teach you more about the printed Word, by using the printed Word within the Holy Bible. No other book can accomplish that. The Holy Bible is the final authority. Any other book read for spiritual growth and direction must lead you back to the Holy Bible or it is leading you astray.

Genuine Christians speak often to God to build their relationship with Him and to free themselves from the bondages caused by the lies within their own mind. *Genuine Christians* also study and become very familiar with the printed pages of the Holy Bible as they feed their spirit and learn to think as God thinks.

If you are a new Christian or if you lack understanding of how to study the Bible, let me make a few simple suggestions that have proven very beneficial to many others including me. First, read the Bible to find out God's plan. Many make the mistake of reading the Bible to *prove their point*. We read the Bible to find God's point and position on things. Reading the Bible to prove your point could possibly lead you astray. When you read the Bible, remain pliable and teachable. Allow the Holy Spirit to show you other scriptures that will reinforce His point within you. Do not shut the door when you sense the Word of God or the Holy Spirit does not agree with your thinking.

When asked, I always suggest that people begin reading the Gospel of John in the New Testament. The Bible's organization is different than we westerners read — chronological, left to right, top to bottom. It is advisable to NOT start in the front and read page for page to the back as you are doing with this book. You will gain much more if you read daily; some of the New Testament, A Psalm and a Proverb as well as a chapter or two from other books in the Old Testament.

The reason I suggest you begin reading the Gospel of John is because it is, in my opinion, the best book of the Bible to understand whom Jesus is. If you gain all the information, facts, and figures of the Bible, but miss out on understanding Jesus, you have missed it all. Jesus is the author and finisher of our faith (Hebrews 12:2). He is the Beginning and the End (Revelation 21:16). He is the payment for all of mankind's sin (1John 2:2). He is the Savior for all who will believe (Titus 2:13, 14). He doesn't ask us to die for Him or His cause, He died for us. No other man has ever done that for mankind (Romans 5:8-9). He is God (Colossians 1:15-18).

Once you have read the Gospel of John a few times, progress on to the book of Acts. This book teaches you how the Holy Spirit worked through the founding Apostles to form the Church. The book of Acts will introduce you more fully to the Holy Spirit and help you understand how He desires and plans to accomplish God's perfect will in your life and in your community. If you miss knowing the Holy Spirit and miss the experiences with Him you miss the power needed to live as, a *genuine* Christian (Acts 1:8).

After you have read Acts and experienced the power and person of the Holy Spirit, follow Him as He leads you through the Scriptures. The Holy Spirit is your teacher (John 14:26) and the Spirit of Truth that will lead you and guide you into all Truth (John 16:13). Therefore, let Him teach you, lead and guide you. He will, most likely, be speaking to you as you continue reading this book.

One more point that may be helpful to you is to obtain a firm understanding of the New Testament before you read the Old Testament. The Old Testament is Jesus concealed, while the New Testament is Jesus revealed. The New Testament gives you the light necessary to more completely understand the Old Testament. The New Testament is the details of the New Covenant, through which our lives currently relate to God and receive His direction. There are wonderful stories of faith and endurance in the Old Testament that you need to read and study, but you will gain so much more by doing so in the light of the New Testament.

Feed yourself, my friends, by reading and meditating on the Holy Bible often.

A Genuine Christian Portrays a Living Hope

"Blessed be the God and Father of our Lord Jesus Christ, who according to His abundant mercy has begotten us again to a living hope through the resurrection of Jesus Christ from the dead." (1Peter 1:3 emphasis added)

The next attribute of a *genuine* Christian is a life that reflects a living hope. We are the most fortunate of all people because our God is ALIVE! No other religion on earth, of which there are several thousand worldwide, can boast that their god or founder is currently alive. The burial location of their founders is well known and most major religions make it mandatory that some sort of pilgrimage occur there, sometime in their lifetime, in order to be pleasing to their god. Well, we know where the author and finisher of our faith was buried. Emphasis on *was*, because He is alive! Jesus doesn't mind if you visit His empty tomb just outside Jerusalem, however, it certainly is not a prerequisite for being *genuine* in our Christian faith or being pleasing to Him. Praise God! Jesus is pleased with us if we are never able to go to Israel and He is pleased with those who are able to go. Going to an empty tomb is not a key to becoming *genuine* in our faith, growing close to God, or growing spiritually. Our God is alive and lives in His followers through His Spirit. Learning to communicate with Him daily is the key to your spiritual growth and maturity.

We serve a living God and our lives should reflect that. In other words, in the middle of the storms of life, those in the world should see us as joyful and peaceful. It's easy to reflect peace when everything is going your way, but what do you reflect when everything is against you?

The world's problems should not be our problems. The world's failures should not be our failures. The world's fears should not be our fears and that, *must* stand out in our life not by what we say, but by how we respond to life's challenges and how we speak about the issues we face. A positive, peaceful response to a bad situation brings hope to all.

Hope is what the world needs and hope is what they are looking for. In fact, another attribute of a *Genuine* Christian is our readiness to explain the hope we have in a respectful and gentle manner. *"But sanctify the Lord God in your hearts, and always be ready to give a defense to everyone who asks you a reason for the hope that is in you, with meekness and fear;"* (1Peter 3:15). If people are not asking, maybe they are not noticing the hope you would like to portray or think you are portraying.

Unfortunately, the wrong things are what too many in the church are noticed for today. Many in the church are just as tormented as those in the world who are living in darkness with no hope at all. For instance — many marriages within the church are in the same kind of trouble as those outside the church. Many within the church are taking antidepressants, sleeping aids, and other types of mood altering drugs easily obtainable these days. This does not need to be. This condition is the result of doing an ineffective job of teaching the Body of Christ how to deal with their inner hurts. My prayer and goal is to help you learn how to eliminate the root cause of your torment. My only desire is to teach and give everyone who is hurting some renewed hope.

In John 14:27, Jesus gives us another promise that should be the primary reason people see the hope within us. Jesus said, *"Peace I leave with you, My peace I give to you; not as the world gives do I give to you. Let not your heart be troubled, neither let it be afraid."*

How does Jesus' peace differ from the world? The world says that we must all agree to be able to live in peace with each other. But Jesus' peace says that you and I can live with perfect inner peace when no one agrees with us. With Jesus' peace, the whole world can be at odds with us and we can still sleep through the storm as Jesus did in Matthew 8:24-27.

Jesus' peace means we can live with no inner turmoil or fear. The difficulties of the world do not need to affect us the way it affects those outside the Body of Christ. Living with the peace of Jesus makes it possible to walk confidently on the troubled seas of life. Living with the peace of Jesus makes it possible to remove, with new invigorated faith, the mountains of opposition from our life. Being *genuine* means, our life will reflect the character and attributes of the author of our faith. Remember? That is our goal, so please do not despair if you are one who is dealing with a life of turmoil or fear. There is hope available to all who want it, right where you sit today.

So, how do we accomplish this lifestyle of peace and hope? Peace and hope comes to us by our relationship with the author of our faith. By living so close and committed to Him we receive and reflect His peace during the storms of life. Inner peace is the result of learning how to bring Jesus into our tumultuous situations so He can be the Lord over them.

Let me share with you a particular time in our life when we were facing some frightful circumstances. In 1989, I was working for a local county government in their information systems department. They hired me as a project leader on some special projects. At the end of the projects the county supervisors were trying desperately to balance their budgets and, as it goes in politics, you are never quite sure of what, who, or when you would be going. The atmosphere was tense and many stood the possibility of losing their jobs. We were personally in a tough financial place at that particular time with two daughters still in high school and we, like everyone else, felt the pressure from the fear of having to look for another job.

Fortunately, the county hired some business consultants who identified the need for a new department. That department would be responsible for managing and coordinating all the hundreds of phones, phone lines, data lines, and related equipment that connected all the employees to each other as well as to the outside world. There were over thirty-five buildings involved and much ongoing change with buildings, employees, and equipment. I just happened to be the one blessed to be offered this challenge. After all, an impossible job is better than no job at all, I reasoned.

I suddenly found myself in a very strange and different world; a technical world I had never been trained for. There was no one to teach me because this department had never actually existed before. Parts of this department were scattered all over the county with other management staff attempting to manage their own little corner of a very big and technically complicated world. I was the first one given the position and authority to actively bring it all together. Some of the players were willing and some, fearing their jobs, actually fought this change, afraid to let anything go for fear they would also be let go.

How do you manage something that really does not exist? How do you learn when no one is willing to teach you? How do you cope with being responsible to aid in planning for the future when you're not even sure what the present should look like? The pressure from the fear of possibly losing a job just doubled, because I now had the pressure of doing what no one there had ever done or look for another job.

Because of all the stress and pressure of the job, I was tempted to join in with the grumblers and complainers — it seemed they were everywhere. I was very tempted to give in to the fear of failing at this new job, a very real possibility, ending up losing my job anyway, but now with the added stress of a failure on my resume. A failure on a technical management resume is not a good sales tool for the future. Something like that could be the end of a very prosperous career in a town of this size and I was not willing to move out of state as so many of my friends had to do. What would you do in these circumstances? I really wanted to cut and run while the getting was good; however, let me tell you what I did.

I had one constant thought on my mind, "I am a servant of the Lord and I serve a big God." Additionally, everyone knew I was a Christian so I understood I was being watched by many I had previously ministered to. Therefore, all of this brought me to one conclusion; I had to act like a servant of God who trusted God for *everything*. I felt that not only my technical reputation was on the line, but how non-believers and young believers I had contact with viewed God was at stake as well. People's future decision about receiving or not receiving Christ as their Lord must be considered when you are facing trials and tests in life. People are watching us and we may be the only Jesus they have ever seen (Romans 8:19). What kind of a Jesus will they see in you? Will they see a powerful Jesus who cares for His followers, or a weak Jesus that can not help His followers through the tough times? Will they see a Jesus that grumbles and complains when the chips are down, or a Jesus that is encouraging and uplifting? You and I carry the responsibility to help them see Jesus as He really is (1John 4:17).

During my first day on the new job, I realized that I had only one hope of accomplishing this task and keeping my job. I needed God's help because everywhere I turned I drew a blank when it came to finding someone who could help me get my arms around this task and begin to make some sense of it. I had people greeting me in the halls with, "Good luck, you're going to need it!" One man even said, "So you're a man who serves God — you better hope He understands county government. You're going to need all the help you can get." By the end of my first day I had a serious talk with God. I said, "Lord, I don't even know what is expected of me. I need you to show me what I am about to miss. I feel like I have been set up to fail. I need you to do my job for me." As I communicated with the Lord I felt His reassuring hand on me and I had an inner knowing that He was about to teach me something I needed to learn. Plus, I suddenly felt like I couldn't lose. I was experiencing the peace that passes all understanding, guarding my heart and mind in Christ Jesus (Philippians 4:7).

From that day on I carried a legal pad and pen with me wherever I went. On the way to and from work, between meetings, from one part of the county to the other, in and out of every building all day long every day I carried my trusty legal pad and a pen because God was forever speaking to me. He would give me people's names I didn't know and when I called them it would always lead me to a task that I needed to be involved in that no one had informed me about. He would alert me of buildings that were being renovated or remodeled, that I needed to be in on the planning and coordinating of, and meetings that I hadn't been invited to. He would give me ideas to present at meetings that solved numerous problems. People in the meetings would ask; "How did you know about that?" I would say, "I didn't, it just came to me." It soon began to look like I had, and I was even accused of having, eyes and ears everywhere within the county buildings and offices. I guess in a way I did, through God's help.

The Lord, from that day on until I resigned to full time ministry three years later, did my job for me. He constantly gave me favor with the men and women I needed in order to make this job and this department a reality. Every lead God gave me yielded fruit that made me a hero to my employer, when all the time it was God who was the real hero. There were many days when I would naturally forget something important, but the Lord would always remind me of it in time for me to respond properly. I became very familiar with the voice of God because I realized only He could do what I was being paid to do and I wasn't afraid to allow Him to do it. This is *Abiding in Christ.*

During the time I worked there, God had many people ask me about the difference they noticed in me or about my ministry. Because of those conversations I was blessed to personally lead over two hundred people to the saving knowledge of Jesus Christ. I never went after them, they all came to me and the Lord did the rest.

To some, it may seem strange to think of allowing God to

actually get involved in your daily routine. The thought of trusting Him with something as important as your employment and the day to day decisions needed for you to excel there may seem a bit daunting. However, let me show you someone else who had an impossible job to accomplish or physically lose his head. You will see that this principle is very biblical and sound. Look with me at the book of Daniel, chapter 2.

If you know the story of Daniel, you will remember that he and three of his friends were taken hostage during the overthrow of Israel by the Babylonian Nation. As prisoners of war, Daniel and his friends were being trained for serving in the Babylonian Kings court (a government job). One day the King did what Kings do, asked his consultants to do the impossible — interpret his dream without telling them what the dream was (Daniel 2:1-9). The wise men, not being that wise, said *"There is not a man on earth who can tell the king's matter; therefore no king, lord, or ruler has ever asked such things of any magician, astrologer, or Chaldean. It is a difficult thing that the king requests, and there is no other who can tell it to the king except the gods, whose dwelling is not with flesh."* And, as the account goes, this made the king go into a rage and he ordered all his wise men killed (Daniel 2:10-13).

However, there was a man named Daniel who was truly a wise-man because he knew that God, the Creator, could and would help him. Daniel, therefore went to the king and asked him for the time to, not only interpret the dream, but to tell the king what his dream was (Daniel 2:14-16). Daniel was given an impossible job to accomplish or, lose everything, including his head. Have you ever been there? Well, Daniel could have done a lot of things, like RUN. But, he didn't because he knew that to run meant he would be running for the rest of his life. He trusted God. I imagine that he figured that if God couldn't help him it wasn't going to be worth hanging around Babylon anyway so let's just get on with it. Well, to make a longer story shorter, Daniel asked God for help to do his job. God did what God always does for people who ask Him in faith believing. He answered Daniel's request and gave him what he needed that night in a dream. The Bible says that when you ask God for wisdom (James 1:5) he ALWAYS gives generously without finding reasons not to give. However, he gives it to us *when we need it* and most of the time it isn't that very instant. Daniel got his wisdom that night in a dream. That means Daniel had to go to bed *trusting* God would answer his request by the time he got to work the next day. If he had a dream, that means he had to sleep. That is truly trusting God, being able to sleep knowing that if you don't perform up to the bosses standard, regardless of how impossible the request, you were going to physically lose your head. Well, God answered, Daniel told the King, and he and his friends were all promoted and Daniel got the big office on the top floor with his windows overlooking the kingdom (Daniel 2:17-49). Please remember this one thing; if God ever did it for anyone else, he will do it for you, if you ask Him and then *trust* Him (John 14:12-14).

I personally believe that if we are ever going to accomplish everything we are destined to accomplish, we will not do it on our own. There seems to be this thing about us humans which forces us to feel we must do it ourselves. That is a lie that constantly holds us back. Once we understand Jesus truly desires to live through us and then allow Him to do so, life becomes enjoyable and exciting. Doing everything for ourselves yields the same fruits as those who do not know God; frustration, fear, worries, ulcers, long days at work, and short hours with our family. How can the fruit of God be produced when we seldom, if ever, call on Him and allow Him to have an active role in our daily lives? Our lives will never reflect our living hope if we do not draw upon the God of living hope in all our circumstances.

We Christians are to be the best there is on the earth at whatever we do for a living. God has called people to be doctors, plumbers, bankers, construction workers, and designers just as sure as He has called apostles, prophets, evangelists, pastors, and teachers. We will never be the best we can be if we feel we alone can do our job; that God is not interested in what we do for a living, or doesn't have the time to get involved with us. God can and will do your job better than you if and when you make the decision to allow Him to help you become the best there is at what you do for a living.

We live in an age that is demanding to see the sons of God. Romans 8:19 says it this way, *"For the earnest expectation of the creation eagerly waits for the revealing of the sons of God."* Sons of God are those who are led by the spirit of God (Romans 8:14). The only hope for the world is Jesus Christ. It is time for His sons to rise to the challenges placed before them and make room for God in their occupation of choice. It is time the world see the living hope God alone provides to all who will call on Him and trust Him alone.

It takes practice to hear the voice of God and to trust that what you are receiving is from God. However, the results are worth every effort it takes. You need only to begin and trust *Him* to teach you how to follow. It is important to have a good understanding of the Word of God because He will never lead you outside the written Word. However, there is one who will, so you must use your knowledge of the Bible to test every spirit (1John 4:1). Once you begin practicing paying more attention to your inner ear, or your heart, you will find out how quickly you can tune out the physical sounds around you. God has much to say about everything in your life. If it affects you, He is interested and will help you when you decide to allow Him.

Knowing He is there and is interested in every detail of your life brings great peace and confidence. A life of inner peace produces hope, joy and the desire to explain to all who ask, why our life is different and filled with hope (1Peter 3:15). And, as your confidence in Him grows, so will the next attribute of *Genuine* Christianity — *genuine* faith.

A Genuine Christian Has Developed Genuine Faith

> *"In this you greatly rejoice, though now for a little while, if need be, you have been grieved by various trials, that the genuine-ness of your faith, being much more precious than gold that perishes, though it is tested by fire, may be found to praise, honor, and glory at the revelation of Jesus Christ."* (1Peter 1:6-7)

Jesus asked His disciples a question when He was teaching them how to pray. In Luke 18:8 Jesus asked, *"Nevertheless, when the Son of Man comes, will He really find faith on the earth?"* Good question. Will He find faith in your life when He comes? The things we have in our possession are not proof of *genuine* faith. No, how we handle the struggles of life proves the genuineness of our faith. In 1Peter 1:6-7 Peter teaches us that faith, like gold, becomes *genuine* as we go through the fire of daily trials and struggles. *Genuine* faith will stand the heat without perishing. Everything that hinders our faith and stands between God and us disappears, as we trust Him and learn to walk more by faith and less by sight. Jesus revealed in you, through exercising *genuine* faith, brings God praise, honor, and glory. Remember, being *genuine* is to *reflect* the character and attributes of the author of our faith.

James 1:2-4 says it this way, "My brethren, count it all joy when you fall into various trials, knowing that the <u>testing of your faith</u> produces patience. But let patience have its perfect work, that you may be perfect and complete, lacking nothing."

James is trying to help us become perfect, or mature, complete, and lacking nothing. That is what all of us want and the only way to get there is through the trials of life. Without trials, there are no victories. Without trials and victories, there is no maturation or promotion from childhood to son-ship.

The goal for every natural child is to grow up and become like his father or older brother. This is a perfect picture of the Christian life. We are all growing toward maturity. We all want our Heavenly Father to be proud of us. We all want to look like our elder brother, Jesus. The way to fulfill this time-honored goal of *genuine* Christianity is by successfully advancing through the struggles of life by learning how to become intimate in our communion, or communication with God.

We must trust Jesus, holding on to Him by communicating with Him and trusting Him to lead us through every struggle. Struggles and trials are the fires of testing that bring out of us known and unknown problems buried deep within our souls.

Our souls (mind) contain the *intellect* as well as our *experiential memory*. Contained within our memory are lies we believe to be true which hold us back. Misinterpretation of life experiences or traumatic events produces lies, or false beliefs. The lies believed cause our emotional pain. Our emotional pain causes us to live more by our feelings than by our faith. Lies believed, hold us back and keep us immature.

We have been instructed to renew our mind in order to become transformed (Romans 12:2), revealing, in us, the likeness of Christ. Renewing our mind works to identify and eliminate the false beliefs. Our intellect, as well as our *experiential memory* can contain false beliefs. However, the lies causing pain, or torments, are always in our experiential memory. Intellectual or cognitive thinking produces no pain.

The first part of Romans 12:2 says, *"Be not conformed to the pattern of the world ..."* In other words, do not respond to the trials of life like those in the world do. They have no hope. They have no understanding of what is taking place internally. They cannot see what you and I see. They have no spiritual perspective. They have no idea of why they are hurting. They have no understanding of faith and how, by faith, the Lord will end their torments.

The second part of Romans 12:2 says " ...but be transformed by the renewing of your mind, that you may prove what is that good and acceptable and perfect will of God." The renewing of the mind is referred to as the saving of our soul in James 1:21 and as the purification of our soul in 1Peter 1:22.

The Bible is not a rulebook of things we are not to do. The Bible is a book of promises that become ours as we connect with God by faith and trust Him to make us mature, complete, lacking nothing (James 1:4). Look for a moment at Peter's second letter, chapter 1, verses 2-4.

> *"Grace and peace be multiplied to you in the knowledge of God and of Jesus our Lord, as His divine power has given to us all things that pertain to life and godliness, through the knowledge of Him who has called us by glory and virtue, by which have been given to us exceedingly great and precious promises, that through these you may be partakers*

> *of the divine nature, having escaped the corruption that is in the world through lust."* (2Peter 1:2-4, emphases added)

Our faith or trust in God produces His promises in our life. When we begin to believe for God's best, by exercising our faith, we can always expect a fight. Your mind will constantly tell you that you are missing it. There will be feelings that this is nuts, not worth it, and impossible. There is always a struggle between the believing and the receiving. Standing firm through the fight and overcoming with our faith is what qualifies us to receive God's best (Hebrews 10:35-36).

Faith levels the playing field, so to speak. If education was God's qualifier, that would eliminate the majority of the world from having a relationship with Him. If God were only accessed by age and wisdom, that too would eliminate the majority of the world. Faith is God's only qualifier. No matter how smart or ignorant you are, no matter how old you are or how young you are, God is there for you through your faith in Him and His Word (Hebrews 11:6).

However, with each promise there are also steps of obedience necessary to qualify you to receive as well. These steps of obedience also put the pressure on us for the good reason of bringing to our attention the need to make some inner, personal changes.

For many, these steps of qualification seem like rules and constraints and therefore, they miss what the Lord is trying to do for them. Rather than giving up, communicate with the Lord about how you feel during these trials of obedience and during the fight of faith. His input will make all the difference in how you get through it all. Remember, He is on your side. He wants you to win and receive His best. His greatest desire is for our success. As you communicate with Him, you are opening the door for Him to teach you His ways in order to bring you into maturity. As you communicate with Him, you are giving Him permission to speak truth to the areas of your mind that currently hold the lies causing your emotional pain. As you communicate with Him, you are giving Him permission to *pull you through* your struggle.

If you will allow me, I want to give you my transliteration to Romans 12:2.

"Do not respond to the trials of life the way the world does but allow me (Jesus) to renew your mind by teaching you as we go through life together. Allow me to speak to your inner pain bringing perfect inner peace and confidence. This process will transform you into everything you have ever wanted to be and into everything I have created you to be. As you allow this experience to take place, you will begin to understand, test and prove my perfect will. Knowing My perfect will is something the whole world wants to know and I will give it to you as you trust me and call on me and experience me through your trials, tests, torments and every fight of faith."

That, my friend is a promise that, when *you allow it* to become fulfilled, will create in you the ability to walk on the stormy seas of life with confidence, to scale the highest mountains and give you the fire-tested *genuine* faith that will cause your mountains to slide into the depths of the sea. All it takes is the willingness to allow God to lead you through the trials of life. Trials come our way whether you follow God or not. However, God turns our trials around to benefit us if we work and communicate with Him. You must work and communicate with God in order to renew your mind. Your confidence in Him will grow as you gain a deeper understanding of what takes place during the renewing of your mind.

A Genuine Christian Relies on God to Renew His or Her Mind

"... but be transformed by the renewing of your mind, that you may prove what is that good and acceptable and perfect will of God" (Romans 12:2).

I wish I had a dollar for every time someone has asked me, "*How do I find God's will for my life.*" This is the major benefit of understanding the total process of mind renewal. Without renewing our mind, we will never find God's will for our life. We will begin to understand God's plan for our life as we begin to know what He knows, think as He thinks and feel what He feels. This is the benefit of renewing the mind. Our *transformation* occurs as our mind is renewed.

As I previously mentioned, there are false beliefs located in our mind, or soul. We have referred to them in many Christian circles as *stinking thinking.* Stinking thinking will always be stinking thinking until you replace it with Truth. Jesus said it this way, *"And you shall know the truth, and the truth will make you free."*

(John 8:32) Free from all the stinking thinking that is holding us back, causing us unnecessary sufferings.

If the truth makes us free then it stands to reason that it must be non-truths or lies residing in our minds that cause us trouble. What we believe either holds us back or propels us forward. Therefore, the only way to move forward is by replacing the lies with the truth. We will discuss how lies got there in the first place as we continue our journey of learning how to become *genuine.* However, please remember, there are two areas of the mind that need renewing and each area is renewed by a different process.

The first is the *cognitive,* or our *intellect.* This is where all the facts and figures we have learned in life are stored. This is the primary section of the mind you work from as you read and study. The second area is the *experiential memory.*

The experiential memory is the section of our mind where we live day to day. The experiential memory contains a detail record of all life's experiences from the womb to the current moment. Every memory contains the following three parts: 1) the mental *Picture* or remembrance of the memory; 2) the *Emotion* experienced during the actual experience; 3) the *Interpretation* of the experience. The interpretation determines whether the memory is peaceful or painful. Lies you believe to be true about self, cause emotional pain.

For now, the most important fact to remember is this; a painful memory is a memory misinterpreted with a lie. It is possible, that during a traumatic event, the interpretation of the memory was accurate at the time, but has since become a lie due to the time and distance from the actual occurrence. For instance: When a child endures abuse, he or she will most likely interpret the experience with something like, *I am in danger and overpowered,* which is a truth. As the child grows up and reaches maturity, the adult may still feel the overwhelming fear of being in danger and overpowered in certain situations. Questions and concerns may arise as loved ones witness this person's childlike, fearful response, to what probably is, to everyone else, a normal day-to-day adult experience. What was once a truth for the child has now become a lie for the adult, due to the time and distance from the original event. Peace for this adult will come as truth replaces the lie believed. We *experience* the truth by communicating with the Spirit of Truth — God.

Both sections of the mind must constantly undergo the renewal process to build your faith and confidence in God to the point of becoming *genuine* – or *"transformed"* as taught in Romans 12:2 and as *"sanctification"* or *"being sanctified by Truth"* in John 17:19.

The church in general has done a very good job of teaching the Word of God and helping us renew the cognitive section of our mind. However, we are falling short when it comes to helping the Body renew the experiential memory section of their mind. The psychiatric and clinical psychology world has been given responsibility for this type of work for the most part. However, according to Dr. Jay E. Adams, Author of *Competent to Counsel*, "Their models of therapy have failed society in the worst possible way. They have never healed anyone according to their own admission and they can give no hope because their models begin and end with man. They fail to take into consideration man's basic relationship to God through Jesus, they neglect God's law, and they know nothing of the power of the Holy Spirit in regeneration and sanctification."[2] They know nothing about Jesus' promise of renewing the mind with truth, freeing us from the painful issues caused by the *stinking thinking* of our life. Total *sanctification* occurs as we exercise our intellect (read, study and memorize) *plus* experience the truth in our pain-filled memories.

The mind always remembers where and how we were hurt. When burned on a stove, your mind will make you very cautious around stoves or anything resembling a stove. To your experiential memory, anything even resembling a stove spells danger. Your memory works the same way in the emotional realm. A lie believed to be true when you were five can cause the adult to respond in a very childish manner because of the bad feelings the lie produces. *Our feelings control us.* Bad feelings make us do bad things or behave badly while good feelings cause us, or allow us, to do good things.

You may be asking, "But if I know better now, as an educated, experienced adult, why do I need to worry about the experience I had when I was five?"

---

[2] Competent To Counsel, Introduction page xviii (P&R Publishing) Dr. Jay E. Adams 1970

Experience always overrides intellectual knowledge during life's daily tests and trials. Our feelings control our actions by instantaneous response, or reflexes before it is possible to access, analyze and respond to our cognitive data. Just like accidentally stumbling into a stove that is off causes you to jump back violently, or overreact, your experiences, good and bad, and the feelings they create within your mind, called emotions, will always drive your responses to life's trials before your intellect will. That is why we act or respond to things in ways we wished we hadn't. Our feelings push us into responding or reacting by automatic emotional reflexes. After we separate from the situation, and take the time to think about it with our intellect, we conclude that we acted improperly.

Until we get our memory renewed by experiencing the Truth (John 8:32), there will remain a distance between what we know cognitively and what we feel experientially. That is why people say things like, "I know what the Word says I am, but I just don't feel like the Word says I should." I have had people say things like this, "Pastor, being a Christian is just too hard. The Word doesn't seem to work for me." In other words, they did not feel what the Word indicated they should feel. For example, we are more than conquerors (Romans 8:37), or I am the righteousness of God in Christ Jesus (2Corinthinans 5:21, etc.). Their *experiential condition* of life did not equal their *position* in Christ.

A pain-filled memory, triggered by their current experience, was overriding their cognitive knowledge. What's the answer to this dilemma? Inner peace comes when our experience equals our cognitive knowledge, or intellect. This only happens as you experience the Truth in the pain-filled memories. You *experience* the Truth as you communicate your current feelings to the Lord. In His communication back to you He will, many times, take you to the pain-filled memory and speak to you about the experience. As you verbally speak what He says, His Truth eliminates the lie.[3] This interaction eliminates your source of pain, which elevates your *experiential condition* to equal your God given *position* as a Christian. There is no remedy created by man that can accomplish this. The only permanent help for inner pain is to receive a spoken Word from the Lord about the lies that are causing the pain.

We have ministered too many who were on medications during the time we dealt with them. One lady in particular came to us with terrible anxieties. She was so bad that she was physically shaking and in one constant panic attack after another. She was experiencing severe drug withdrawals, and for the first time in over thirty years, she was feeling the fear masked by her medication. From infancy through her late teens, her father and her grandfather sexually abused her. There was no safe place for her. She was in a constant state of fear and terror. During college, her school counselors helped her find a psychiatrist who immediately put her on a drug that masked her fear. Unfortunately, it took every other feeling away with it. She felt healed of the fear. However, just before she came to see us she discovered she was pregnant and there-

---

[3] For scriptural understanding of why we must speak what the Lord speaks to us, refer to Appendix I, *Why We Must Speak Audibly To God.*

fore taken off the pain-numbing drug.

The psychiatrist got angry with her as she complained how her body and her mind felt off the medication. "It is time you begin thinking of someone besides yourself; after all, you now have an unborn baby to consider" they said. No one explained to her how her body would feel or what fear would once again feel like. This abrupt rejection from her doctor is precisely what she did not need because it reinforced many other negative feelings she was suffering from. This rejection from a frustrated caregiver totally put her into a tailspin of self-destruction. However, it did force her to seek additional help, which brought her to us.

Once the Holy Spirit began speaking to her pain-filled memories, her fears went away. She suddenly began feeling what life should really feel like. It had been years since she really felt happy or excited. She had been totally numb because of two little tablets taken every day of her life while the source of the pain remained in her mind.

> *"And you shall know the truth and the truth shall make you free."* (John 8:32)

The word "*know*" in this scripture is <u>not</u> talking about knowledge gained through the intellect. The Greek word "*ginosko,*" translated "*know*" means "Knowledge gained by experience." (Strong's #1097) The word "*truth*" is translated from the Greek word "*alëtheia*" which means, "The reality pertaining to an appearance," in other words, an experience. (Strong's #225) We must *experience* the Truth before it can free us. To know cognitively through reading and studying *feeds us.* Experiencing it first hand through our communication with the Lord (Truth) *frees us.* Freedom comes as the truth received destroys the lies found in our experiential memory creating *transformation by the renewing of your mind* (Romans 12:2b).

Another question many people have when considering the memories of the past is, *"Why didn't these problems get resolved and renewed when I got born again?"*

When you receive Jesus as your Savior, you must go to the cross for the forgiveness of your sins committed. Our emotional pain is caused either by misinterpretations of experiences or by others who have sinned against us. That creates a wound that needs to be healed — not a sin that needs forgiven.

Abusive behavior of others generally causes the abused to believe lies about themselves and stays buried in the subconscious long after the event occurred. This again is not sin of our doing and only the truth from the One who is Truth can heal us making us free.

Let me share with you a testimony of a young lady we will call "Alice". A concerned friend of hers brought Alice to us many years ago. She was born again but still filled with so much shame and self-loathing that she could not look anyone in the eye. She rarely left her house or visited with anyone in the neighborhood. The only time she would communicate with anyone was if one of her concerned neighborhood friends caught her outside. When others would talk to her, she would never look them in the face or allow them to see her face. She constantly was looking down at her feet with her hair hanging down over her face. When she came into our office, she had her head in her sweatshirt and she refused to look at us when we talked to her. Her neighbors were concerned for her because she began to show signs of physically harming herself.

As we ministered to her, we found out that every male had sexually abused her in her life from a very young age until she finally escaped her home as an older teenager. The men's sins perpetrated upon her filled her with shame and feelings of being dirty and disgusting. What these men did to her had, of course, absolutely nothing to do with her value and cleanliness as a child of God. After all, she was a victim. However, like most abuse victims, she could not rid herself of the shameful feelings and she hated herself for it.

Follow along as I recount a short segment of the ministry time we had with her:

> PL. Looking at Alice with her head in sweatshirt I asked, "Do you want to take your head out of your shirt so we can talk?"
>
> Alice.*She mumbled something I couldn't hear while she shook her head no.*
>
> PL. That's ok. We only want to help you. Will you tell me what you are feeling?
>
> Alice.Dirty and yucky.
>
> PL. Lord Jesus, would you show Alice where this dirty, yucky feeling is coming from?

When the Lord shows you a memory just tell me how old you are, where you are at and whom you are with in the memory. She began to weep and sob heavily so I asked her, "Will you tell me how old you are in the memory?"

> Alice.I am seven and my father is hurting me sexually.

PL. What feels true about you in that memory?

Alice.I feel dirty.

PL. Lord is there some truth you can give Alice about her feeling in this memory. Alice, when the Lord speaks to you it will be a gentle knowing or understanding. What is Jesus saying to you?

Alice.I see Jesus in my memory. He said it was not my fault and I am clean. I see myself in white clothes. What does that mean?

PL. I read Revelations 3:18 to her; "I counsel you to buy from me gold refined in the fire, that you may be rich; and white garments, that you may be clothed, that the shame of your nakedness may not be revealed ..."
What do you feel now?

Alice.*I feel better.* (She still had her face covered with her shirt and her long hair.)

PL. Lord if there is another memory she needs to see to help her, would you please show her now? Now, tell me if another memory comes to you. She suddenly began to weep again with an intensity I had never, to that point, experienced. (I have since learned that type of reaction is called an "abreaction"; the release of a repressed or forgotten emotion.) Alice, will you tell me what you are seeing? You are going to be ok, it's just a memory but please stay in it until Jesus speaks to you. What are you seeing?

Alice.*It's terrible! I'm dirty! I'm awful! How could I have done that? I'm yucky!* (She was almost screaming this as she was crying, and sobbing, pulling her hair, banging her head against the wall.)

PL. How old are you in the memory Alice?

Alice.*I'm ten and my stepfather is forcing me to have sex with a dog while he and his friends laugh at me.* (Revealing this information came accompanied by more screaming and banging her head against the wall.)

PL. Jesus, is there some truth you can give Alice about this memory? Tell me what Jesus says.

Alice.I don't want to hear from Jesus!

PL. Why not?

Alice.He hates me because of what I did. I don't want to see him!

PL. Jesus, is that true? Do you hate Alice for what this little ten-year-old girl did? Now tell me what Jesus' answer is.

Alice.He said; "No, I don't hate you. I love you. What happened to you was not your fault. You are my daughter now. Now, I can protect you. I have made you clean. I love you and will never leave you alone." Her sobbing and banging her head stopped and she looked at my wife and I for the first time and said, "Could that be true?"

PL. What do you feel now?

Alice. I feel good. It's all gone. I don't feel dirty and yucky any more. Could that be true?

PL. Does it feel true?

Alice. Yes. Yes it does! It's all gone. I feel good for the first time. Am I going to be ok?

PL. I think you are ok. Don't you? (Alice jumped to her feet and gave her friend and my wife a hug and then shook my hand, looked me straight in the eye and said: *"Thank you! I cannot remember ever feeling good like this in my entire life. Thank you! I think I love you all, I'm not sure, but love must feel something like this. Doesn't it?"*

That was a part of our first session with Alice. It took three additional sessions of about two hours each to help her find the peace she needed to carry on in life. She is now in a good church, married and has several children. When Jesus spoke truth to her in her pain-filled memories, she instantly lost all sense of shame and self-loathing. She suddenly could see herself wearing garments of white. She told us that Jesus showed her how precious she was and from that moment on, she began to like herself. By the end of our first meeting, she never looked down again. She looks others in the eye and carries on communication like a child of God should. She said, "I thought everybody could see my filth so I couldn't look them in the eye. When my pastor told me I was the righteousness of God because I had accepted Jesus (her position), I felt that God had discarded me because of how I still felt (her life condition). After all, how could God love something as dirty as I was?"

That misfortunate young lady felt that if she punished herself enough she could pay for what had happened to her and then maybe Jesus would take the feelings away. She truly believed that Jesus was mad at her, after all, she reasoned, I should have stopped it. (It is my experience that a child will endure horrible things from a parent and still protects the parent as well as feels responsible for not stopping it; even though a child cannot nor will they stop a parent or adult, from carrying out whatever sick activities they perpetrate upon them.)

Misinterpreting our experiences is one way we ingest lies. However, some have believed lies about themselves because those who should have been trusted to help them interpret their experiences correctly convinced them the lie was the truth. For instance, all abusers work to convince their victims that they, the victims, are to blame for the abuse. During or following the abuse, the perpetrators make statements such as: "You made me do it.", "I couldn't help myself because you made me do it.", "If you weren't so bad I wouldn't have to get so mean with you.", "If you weren't so beautiful I wouldn't have lost control.", "If you would behave mommy wouldn't have to hurt you."

The misinterpretations of experiences are part of the human experience and that is why it is so important to learn how to communicate with the Lord moment by moment in life. Only the Holy Spirit can help us accurately interpret each experience. Our mind always interprets our experiences based upon the premise of, *"What does this experience make me feel about myself."* Your mind will always accuse you of being wrong or cause you to believe it was your entire fault. Only the Holy Spirit will deliver truth about each experience of life. If we need correction because of our improper behavior, the Holy Spirit will gently help us see our error without belittling us.

The trials or fires of life bring to the surface our character flaws and our false beliefs, opening us to receive truth. By paying attention to the bad feelings we have been running from, we, with God's help, can identify the lies that are producing feelings, which cause our improper actions, holding us back in our spiritual growth. Getting the lies replaced with Truth creates *genuine* faith within us, one of the most important and powerful attributes clearly seen in the *genuine* Christian. The good news is you can relax, enjoy and trust the Lord while He helps eliminate all the past reasons for your current pain. You can also rest assured; the Lord will also be on guard to help you interpret each new experience with truth giving you a brighter, peace-filled future. Your only responsibility is to pay attention to that gentle inner voice, responding to Him, keeping yourselves in His perfect peace. He will help you *gird up the loins of our mind* to give you a life of rest and peace.

The Genuine Christian Lives A Life of Rest and Peace

> *"Therefore gird up the loins of your mind, be sober, and rest your hope fully upon the grace that is to be brought to you at the revelation of Jesus Christ:"* (1Peter 1:13)

> *"Come to Me, all you who labor and are heavy laden, and I will give you rest."* (Matthew 11:28)

All through Jesus' earthly ministry, He called everyone to Himself to receive His peace and rest. Now, as our Advocate at the right hand of the Father, He continues to call us, by the Holy Spirit, into His peace (John 14:27) and rest (Hebrews 4). God's plan from the beginning was to carry His children's burdens and heal their sorrows and broken hearts. During Jesus' first public ministry appearance, at the synagogue in Nazareth, He read the words of Isaiah, declaring their fulfillment for the first time that day. *"The Spirit of the Lord is upon Me, because He has anointed Me to preach the gospel to the poor; He has sent Me to heal the brokenhearted, To proclaim liberty to the captives and re-*

covery of sight to the blind, To set at liberty those who are oppressed; To proclaim the acceptable year of the Lord" (Luke 4:18, 19; Isaiah 61:1-2). Neither His desire nor His plans have changed (Hebrews 13:8). He is still healing the brokenhearted, setting captives free and carrying the burdens of the oppressed, when you call on Him and learn how to work with Him.

Life can become very stressful when you find yourself alone. Many Christians think they have the Lord's help, when in fact; they are unknowingly going it alone. One such area is how they deal with their feelings. Most people, unfortunately, favor denying or ignoring their feelings. Denial is not an option Jesus will approve of however. He desires to take us to freedom and that means we may need to go to where it hurts occasionally.

In prayer one day, the Lord impressed the following three thoughts on my mind:

1. Identifying your feelings improves your communication with God. It brings you closer to God as you learn to cast all your cares upon Him and it increases your confidence in God by building your faith as you learn to trust Him to help you with those negative feelings.
2. Ignoring your feelings hardens your heart and shuts down communication with God or eliminates the primary opportunity we have to communicate with Him.
3. Living by your feelings drives you from God as you allow your feelings to become your guide.

Many think that by ignoring their feelings they have successfully stopped them from guiding or driving them. However, the truth is, our feelings do drive us. The more we work to cope with or ignore them, the more they actually control us.

Many are ignoring their feelings because they misunderstand the purpose of emotions. Emotional pain is simply God's method of alerting us to the fact that there is a lie we believe to be true about ourselves. This lie separates us from God. Have you noticed that everything that separates us from God feels bad while only peace and joy come from our time of communing with or sitting in the presence of God (Psalm 16:11)? When we believe lies about our self, it feels bad. A lie is always the opposite of what God says about us. God establishes ALL truth about everything. There is no such thing as relative truth.

Lies build walls between God and us. For those who have been born again (Christians) the lie is the seed of sin. As Christians, our sin nature has been made inoperable, destroying the power that sin had over us before we were born again (Romans 6:6 and Colossians 2:11).

That being true, what then causes Christians to misbehave or sin? The lies they believe to be true causes them to sin because of the inner pain the lie creates. Look for a moment at Adam and Eve's experience. We all know that Eve sinned against God, but why? How did sin get into a perfect world? Look at Genesis 3 with me for a moment.

"Now the serpent was more cunning than any beast of the field which the Lord God had made. And he said to the woman, 'Has God indeed said, 'You shall not eat of every tree of the garden'?' And the woman said to the serpent, 'We may eat the fruit of the trees of the garden; but of the fruit of the tree which is in the midst of the garden, God has said, 'you shall not eat it, nor shall you touch it, lest you die.' Then the serpent said to the woman, 'You will not surely die. For God knows that in the day you eat of it your eyes will be opened, and you will be like God, knowing good and evil.'" So when the woman saw that the tree was good for food, that it was pleasant to the eyes, and a tree desirable to make one wise, she took of its fruit and ate. She also gave to her husband with her, and he ate. Then the eyes of both of them were opened. .... they heard the sound of the Lord God walking in the garden in the cool of the day, and Adam and his wife hid themselves from the presence of the Lord God ... " (Genesis 3:1 – 7a, 8).

Eve did not sin until she chose to act on the lie, "*You will not surely die.*" Whether she believed the lie or just wanted to believe it, the result was the same. When she saw that the tree could make her become like God, only then did she act against God, which is sin. The devil deceived her by playing on her misunderstanding of the phrase, "You shall not die." Once Eve believed the lie that she was not good enough, she sinned by taking the action promised to make her like God.

Again, our emotional pain comes from believing lies about oneself. Bad feelings cause us to do bad things. Emotional pain is God's warning system that alerts us when something is in our soul that will separate us from Him. Even grief and sorrow can effectively separate us from God. That danger is why God's Word tells us, *"He is despised and rejected by men, A man of sorrows and acquainted with grief . . . Surely He has borne our grief And carried our sorrows"* (Isaiah 53:3a, 4a).

When my first grandchild was born, we watched him fight for life for two days before he went home to be with Jesus. Our grief and sorrow was suffocating. Our faith in God was weakening through all the inner pain. I asked the Lord why he had to die and He spoke the same thing in two different ways to my wife and me. To me He said, "It is not for you to know at this time. Your grandson is with me. You will have eternity with him." When I received that word from God, all my grief and sorrow left. Subconsciously I must have believed I would never be able to see or enjoy him again. I was able to go on living, knowing I have more reasons now than ever to look forward to going home to not only see Jesus but my first grandchild as well. When my wife asked God the same basic question in her time of grief, He simply gave her a Scripture reference. She immediately looked up Deuteronomy 29:29, *"The secret things belong to the Lord our God, but those things which are revealed belong to us and to our children forever, that we may do all the words of this law."* As it did with me, her grief and sorrow immediately left. That word gave her the strength to go on. She knew that God was aware of her pain and that He cared. Grief and sorrow can taint our memories of those whom we have lost. Many times, we have seen people who grieved so long that just the mention of their loved one caused them to weep uncontrollably.

God wants to carry your grief and your sorrow but you must allow Him to do that. As you speak to Him about what you are feeling, you are also giving Him permission to enter that area of your life and heal you by carrying those feelings. When grief and sorrow lift, you instantly get a fresh new view of the one being grieved and their memory suddenly becomes sweet again. Some grieve because they feel abandoned and all alone. When this happens, the Lord is always very willing to encourage the one grieving that He is still with them and they are not alone.

The lie that keeps many from receiving this revelation is the belief that bad feelings are a sign of weakness. Nothing could be further from the truth. Again, bad feelings are an indication God is trying to help you clear out something that stands between you and Him.

Another lie that many believe is feelings are the "*feminine side*" of their brain, or "*right brain thinking*". In other words, men are not supposed to feel and if they do, it is *un-natural.* That is pure Freudian nonsense. This type of thinking keeps men in total bondage, fearful of admitting they have feelings at all. Jesus does not want your feelings to have control over you any more than you do. However, you would be dead if you had no feelings. Jesus' desire and plan is that you give those feelings to Him so He can replace them with His peace by speaking truth to you. This occurs through our verbal communication with the Lord. As you allow Him to help you with the everyday feelings, you are strengthening your faith and confidence in Him.

Bad feelings cause you to protect and justify yourself by blaming others. Bad feelings are what you are running from. Have you noticed you can't run fast enough or far enough to lose them? The Holy Spirit is saying, *"Therefore we also, since we are surrounded by so great a cloud of witnesses, let us lay aside every weight, and the sin which so easily ensnares us, and let us run with endurance the race that is set before us, looking unto Jesus, the author and finisher of our faith ... "* (Hebrews 12:1,2a).

With your permission my paraphrase goes like this: Come on, there are a lot of people watching us so let Me help you identify and throw off the weights or heavy burdens caused by anger, fear, and other destructive feelings. Those bad feelings slow you down and hold you back, causing you to sin when you are trying so hard to be good. The only way we can run this race with endurance is by looking at and going to Jesus, the author and finisher of our faith.

Going through life with emotional pain is like running a race with lead weights hanging on your feet. No matter how much energy you burn and no matter how hard you try, others still easily pass you. Working with the Lord by submitting your pain to Him and allowing Him to speak truth to your issues removes the lead weights and makes running your race easy and enjoyable. Running from your pain by refusing to admit you are hurting is refusing the type of life (John 10:10) Jesus came to provide us. ZOE is the Greek word for *life in the spirit — the God kind of life.* Unfortunately, running from inner pain has become more common than being free and able to run the race peacefully. The world is so filled with inner pain, it is rare to find someone who is actually free to be themselves and at peace with themselves and with God.

Thank God for Jesus' offer. "*Come to Me, all who labor and are heavy laden, and I will give you rest*" (Matthew 11:28). The feelings we are dealing with become heavy burdens that weigh us down making life painful and laborious. The fear caused by the constant pressure of being exposed can be suffocating and dehabilitating, making us stumble and fall as we struggle to follow Jesus. The good news is Jesus has rest for us as we learn how to give Him our turmoil and fears.

It is not Jesus' intention for our Christian walk to be hard work. Jesus continues in Matthew 11:29 *"Take My yoke upon you and learn from me, for I am gentle and lowly in heart, and you will find rest for your souls."* When we communicate our feelings to Jesus, rather than wrestle with or run from them, Jesus has promised we will learn or receive something from Him. What we receive are the truths that will put to rest or destroy the lies that make us feel so bad. Blaming others for your inner pain and turmoil never resolves anything. Running from your inner turmoil does not bring us peace and rest. The blame game and running from our issues only adds to the burden and pain.

Coping mechanisms do not bring us peace and rest. We have many years of history that proves coping with, abstaining from, or running from inner pain is not the peace and rest Jesus promises (John 14:27, 16:33).

Eminent psychiatrists have become disillusioned. In 1955,

the American Psychiatric Association held a symposium on "Progress in Psychiatry." Here is the sort of statement which appeared in the published accounts: "Psychotherapy is today in a state of disarray almost exactly as it was 200 years ago."[4] In an address to the A.P.A. the next year, 1956, Percival Bailey said: "The great revolution in psychiatry has solved few problems ... One wonders how long the hoary errors of Freud will continue to plague psychiatry."

Patients, failing to recover after years of analysis and thousands of dollars later, have also been wondering about the boasts of psychiatry. Some, getting worse, have begun to suspect that many of their problems are treatment induced. H. J. Eysenck, Director of the University of London's Department of Psychology, recently wrote: 'The success of the Freudian revolution seemed complete. Only one thing went wrong. The patients did not get any better."[5]

We have over two hundred years of history proving that the coping mechanism of clinical counseling, using the model provided us by psychology, cannot heal emotional pain. That is why we see the flood of mood-altering drugs in our society

---

[4] Zilboorg, G., in Mowrer, The Crisis in Psychology (Princeton: Van Nostrand, 1961), p. 3.
[5] Dr. Jay E. Adams, *Competent to Counsel* P&R Publishing Company, 1970

today. I believe it is also the reason we see such increase in the use of illegal drugs in our society today as well. People are trying desperately to escape their pain.

Drug usage, legal or illegal, (including alcohol and smoking) is a coping mechanism. Drugs do not heal or correct the problem. The purpose of a mood-altering drug is to cover or mask the pain in order to make life more bearable, or cope-able, for those suffering. All too often, those same mood-altering drugs cause additional problems for those suffering, such as physical damage to the body, hallucinations, and addictions. For instance, antidepressants causing suicidal thoughts often resulting in permanent physical damage or death, especially in children and very young adults is a well-documented fact today.

The process of psychological counseling identifies the cause of the inner turmoil so the one suffering can transfer his or her pain to the person or persons originally responsible. This is a cognitive transference rather than an emotional one and is another lie that just complicates the torment. Mental transference to another human being does not heal or bring peace. It is an attempt at coping, not curing. Physical transference of your pain to another human is what witchcraft and sorcery do. This does not heal or bring peace. It simply does not work.

God is the only one who has a transference program that heals. Consider with me God's counsel of casting all your care upon Him, or transferring all your cares upon Him knowing He cares for us (1Peter 5:7). How about, "Be anxious for nothing, but in all your pain and turmoil, tell me, being thankful knowing I will take it from you and guard your intellect and your soul with my peace." (Philippians 4:6 author's paraphrase) Another good one is, "Come on, enter my rest because I have a word for you that will heal you. I know everything about you and you don't have to explain yourself to me. I have been where you are and tempted as you are with the same emotional pains of rejection, fear, shame, and frustration. I can help you by taking all that stuff on for you, so, come on in to My throne of grace where you will find My mercy and receive all the grace you need for this time of need" (Hebrews 4:11-16, author's paraphrase).

This is the guarantee God's transference program works every time. "Surely He has borne our griefs and carried our sorrows yet we esteemed Him stricken, smitten by God and afflicted. But He was wounded for our transgressions, He was bruised for our iniquities; the chastisement for our peace was upon Him, and by His stripes we are healed." (Isaiah 53:3-5, emphasis added.) This pain transference program that we are talking about always brings healing and perfect inner peace. This is what Psychology tries to emulate, but God, being the author and finisher of pain transference through Jesus, is the only one who can make it work.

There is an even greater danger with coping than missing your healing, as if that's not bad enough. Once again, all coping, which includes all maintenance programs, emotional medication regiments, and psychological counseling, creates *apathy*. Apathy is not feeling, not caring, being indifferent to the situation. Apathy is the beginning of and the process of *spiritual death*. Anything that keeps you from turning to Jesus is increasing the wall between you and Him rather than destroying it. Spiritual growth, the opposite of apathy, is growing closer to the Lord not turning from or blocking us from Him.

Hebrews 4:1 and 10 says "Therefore, since a promise remains of entering His rest, let us fear lest any of you seem to have come short of it. . . . For he who has entered His rest has himself also ceased from his works as God did from His."

I believe the works that the author of Hebrews is referring

to is the constant effort to perfect and protect ourselves. It is constantly coping or wrestling with life issues that Jesus has promised to give us rest from by carrying for us. Have we fallen as victims to the same work, work, work, attitude the Church in Galatia did?

"This only I want to learn from you: Did you receive the Spirit by the works of the law, or by the hearing of faith? Are you so foolish? Having begun in the Spirit, <u>are you now being made perfect by the flesh?</u> ...Therefore He who supplies the Spirit to you and works miracles among you, does He do it by the works of the law, or by the hearing of faith? ... . But that no one is justified by the law in the sight of God is evident, for the just shall live by faith" (Galatians 3:2, 3, 5, 11).

The sooner we quit working at fixing our own problems and running from our inner pain and begin trusting Jesus' plan, the sooner we enter His rest, become *genuine*, and will only then begin to fulfill the great commission.

The Genuine Christian Lives A Holy Life

"Be holy, for I am holy." (1Peter 1:16)

The next attribute on our way to becoming *genuine* is found in 1Peter 1:15. *"But as He who called you is holy, you also be holy in all your conduct."* The writer of the letter to the Hebrew Christians said it this way. *"Pursue peace with all people, and holiness, without which, no one will see the Lord"* (Hebrews 12:14).

I have heard it said that, how we behave when no one is looking determines our personal level of holiness. I think this is probably true. Anyone can put on a good presentation for short periods. Too many of us, church leaders included, are guilty of assuming that a good presentation during church services and public gatherings prove a mature, holy life when away from church. If you really want to know the level of holiness, a person is living, check in on them during their tough trials of life when they think no one is around. A *genuine* Christian will be transparent. A *genuine* Christian will be the same during all phases of life. No matter what is going on in their life they will prove to have *genuine* faith and display a life of hope and maturity that runs much deeper than the surface; deeper than any mask can portray or cover.

The truth is we are never alone. "And there is no creature hidden from His sight, but all things are naked and open to the eyes of Him to whom we must give account" (Hebrews 4:13). Being holy is being mature in the Lord. Being holy means we are more fearful of and concerned about bringing reproach upon the Lord than obtaining some temporary pleasure by seeking immediate gratification for ourselves. Jesus says, "If anyone desires to come after Me, let him deny himself, and take up his cross, and follow Me. For whoever desires to save his life will lose it, but whoever loses his life for My sake will find it." (Matthew 16:24, 25 emphasis added) Living a holy life proves we are more concerned with how the Lord sees us than what others may think about us. "Knowing that you were not redeemed with corruptible things, like silver or gold, from your aimless conduct received by tradition from your father, but with the precious blood of Christ, as a lamb without blemish and without spot" (1Peter 1:18, 19, emphasis added).

Being holy is not the price we pay for our salvation. Being holy is honoring the price He paid for our salvation.

Peter said, "*...you also be holy in all your conduct ...*" and all your conduct means ALL your conduct. In the electronic, instantaneous, technological age in which we live, we can get ourselves into more trouble than we can ever hope to get ourselves out of if we don't watch it. For instance, more and more people are becoming addicted to pornography and gambling because it is so easily accessible right in the privacy of your own home. You no longer have to go to some sleazy magazine rack or low rent bookstore to find unsuitable images to satisfy your lustful curiosity. You no longer have to go to some smoke-filled back room to try your luck (Or should I say, misfortune?) at gambling. Now you just turn on your computer or TV and within an instant, you can have the entire underworld of illicit-sex and gambling at your disposal.

You think it won't hurt anyone, but it hurts you and will eventually hurt your relationships. The illicit images you have imprinted on your memory will haunt you when you least expect them or want them to, and they will continue to haunt you far into your future. They are not something you can just turn on and off at will. They become a wall *you* erect between you, God, and His plan for you. They will be a door *you* open up to unclean spirits and lustful passions that should remain dormant in every human. There is no such thing as just peeking, no harm done. I have ministered to sex abusers as well as to the sexually abused, and there is always one thing in common with all the cases — there was always pornography involved somehow. The idea that "no one gets harmed" is the first lie you must allow God to deal with. Ask Him if no one gets hurt.

> *"Therefore gird up the loins of your mind, be sober, and rest your hope fully upon the grace that is to be brought to you at the revelation of Jesus Christ."* (1Peter 1:13)

Living a holy life means you will be calling on the Lord regularly as you go through life. Living holy does not cost us, it adds to our abilities as it allows us to share in the life and power of Jesus Christ.

As you call upon the Lord with the issues that would keep you from living a holy life, Jesus will reveal His character and strength to you. By His grace, He will show you His way of dealing with each issue of life. He will help develop your character by strengthening you against the temptations. He will also show you why the temptations are so powerful, where, when and how you received the lie, and then give you the truth that will free you from it.

The thought established in verse 13 continues with the next verse which says, *"as obedient children, not conforming yourselves to the former lusts, as in your ignorance"* (1Peter 1:14). You and I will either live according to the *ignorance* of our days before we were born again or we will live by the revelation of Jesus Christ. The choice is ours. If we continue to live as in our ignorant days, we are giving in to firmly established habits. Making new, holy habits are the only way to break old unholy habits. Calling on the Lord in our time of temptation is a holy habit. I like the way the Phillips translation puts verse 14.

> *"Live as obedient children before God. Don't let your character be molded by the desires of your ignorant days."* (1Peter 1:14, J.B. Phillips Translation)

Unmet emotional needs that you are trying to meet in ungodly ways are, much of the time, the cause of addictive, compulsive behaviors. Addictive, compulsive behavior can also be the result of an emotional wound that needs healed, such as a lack of affirmation, a sense of abandonment, trapped, being overwhelmed, etc. Regardless of the cause, only God can meet the deepest emotional needs of mankind and only God can heal the emotional wounds caused by man. It doesn't matter if your addictions are drug/alcohol, gambling, sex, work, or church it is all unholy, the cause is always emotional and the answer is always God.

Yes, you can be addicted to attending church, going to meetings, conferences, even work. People addicted in this way are running or hiding from something. For instance, years ago,

I found myself working fourteen to sixteen hour days as a normal schedule — driven to work all the time. When I wasn't working, I was thinking about my work. Years later I found out that fear of failure was driving me, caused by believing that I was inadequate. I believed that if I was going to make it I had to work twice as hard as everyone else did. I, of course, justified it by blaming my actions and schedule on my family saying, "I'm only doing this for you so you can have everything you want." This too, was a lie I eventually had to confront. In the end, the emotional wound of inadequacy that was driving me, God eventually spoke to and healed, as I will share with you later in this book.

We have ministered to many others who were running from situations at home and their only refuge, in their mind, was going to church or Christian conferences. It made them feel better about themselves and they truly believed that their actions pleased God. They finally had to face the fact that all it was doing was keeping them from confronting the issues they had at home.

In one church I served during my pastorate, there was a lady, who never missed a meeting. I don't care what time the meeting was, she was there. If we had an all night meeting, she was there all night. If we had had a marathon, she would have been there through the entire thing. In the end, I found out that her husband and family were anti-church because she was always there and never home. When I confronted her about it, with the hopes of winning her family, she told me her husband was a bit abusive so she just stayed at church all the time.

Running away is not a responsible way to address problems. Running away did not please God, and it did not help her husband. Confronting him with concern and love did. Avoiding your issues is unholy behavior called apathy. Holy living or *genuine* Christianity is responsibly confronting your issues with God's direction and help.

God has the only answer to these problems. We have worked with all of these addictive behaviors at one time or another. The base problem is always the same and the healing answer is always from God. For many years, I smoked three packs of cigarettes per day and an occasional cigar just to sweeten up the atmosphere. I also was an alcoholic that thought I had control of it, until I attempted to quit. Plus, I have already mentioned that during that period I was a workaholic. Let me share with you the simplicity of how I worked with God to eliminate this addictive behavior in my life.

My first step was to admit I had a problem. Deep in our hearts, we know if we have a problem. Or better yet, we know when the problem has us. If you think it will take care of itself, you need to rethink it. It never takes care of itself, no matter how vehemently you deny you have a problem. Deep down inside you know it and the sooner you can admit it the sooner healing will occur.

The next step is then to eliminate shame, the main reason we humans do not turn to God in the first place. Our shame and guilt makes us believe that God is angry and disappointed with us. You must reach the point where you understand and believe God is not mad at you or disappointed in you (Jeremiah 29:11). God, knowing the beginning from the end, knew you were going to fall long before you ever knew Him. He understands your particular situation and is ready to help you out of it the moment you are ready to admit you need His help. Just speak to Him, "Lord, are you disappointed in me?" and then listen quietly inside for a few seconds. The first impression or *gentle knowing* is from God. If you want to test it to see if it was God and I always do, then speak it out loud. If it makes you feel better or changes your feelings, it was from God. If the response belittles you or causes more guilt, it was not God. Tell your mind to be still and merely ask Him again. Don't think it. Speak it out loud. Every time God speaks to you, you must speak it out loud before it will ever do you any good.[6]

Once you have opened your communication with God on the issue, just ask Him why you are obsessed with whatever it is that has you trapped. He will tell you or He will show you a memory of where the emotional issue of your life began.

All emotional pains have an origin and cause just like all physical pain. The cause of your emotional pain is located in a memory (the origin) that has been misinterpreted. The lie or misinterpretation of the event is the source of your pain. The Lord will show you the memory that holds this lie when you ask Him to help you understand where your current bad feelings are coming from — He wants to speak truth to you and make you free.

Some people have great difficulty understanding why everything resides in their memory, or their past. The simple answer is, because everything resides in your past. ***The current moment is always fleeting by***. I highlighted that last statement

---

[6] For a scriptural understanding of why we need to speak to God aloud, refer to Appendix I.

just to emphasize that the statement is now in your memory. You must remember it or go back and relive (reread) that statement in order to recall it. If you have misinterpreted anything during the reading of this book that too, must be corrected by looking back a little ways or accessing your memory.

It seems some Christians are afraid of their memory, potentially because of one scripture in Philippians. I make this statement because of some opposition I have faced when trying to help hurting Christians. Many quote this scripture when I tell them that the Lord will show them a memory.

> *"Brethren, I do not count myself to have apprehended; but one thing I do, forgetting those things which are behind and reaching forward to those things which are ahead..."* (Philippians 3:13)

The Apostle Paul made that statement within the context of comparing his past religious life of works and all of his accomplishments with this new freedom, found only by faith in Jesus Christ.

> *"But these things were gain to me, these I have counted loss for Christ. Yet indeed I also count all things loss for the excellence of the knowledge of Christ Jesus my Lord, for whom I have suffered the loss of all things, and count them as rubbish, that I may gain Christ and be found in Him, not having my own righteousness, which is from the law, but that which is through faith in Christ, the righteousness which is from God by faith; that I may know Him and the power of His resurrection, and the fellowship of His sufferings, being conformed to His death, if, by any means, I may attain to the resurrection from the dead."* (Philippians

3:7-11,emphasis added)

In other words, Paul was not willing to hold on to the accomplishments of his past, but was eagerly looking forward (as we all should) to the new accomplishments God would be doing through him, making it possible for him to experience God's power. Looking at situations in our memory is simply having our mind renewed, which Paul also taught us in Romans 12:1-2.

Your past is the only thing that can separate you from what God desires to do in and through your life (Romans 8:38, 39). Your past formed all of your beliefs (truths and lies). The lies you believe will constantly fight against you as you live life. That is why God instructs us to present our bodies (our life) on the altar of God as a *living sacrifice* in the process of renewing our mind (Romans 12:1-2).

Mind renewal is more than cognitively gathering more information. There is no sacrifice or pain involved in gathering facts and learning. You will not have your mind completely renewed unless you are willing to, metaphorically, *stay on the altar.*

> *"I beseech you therefore, brethren, by the mercies of God, that you present your bodies a living sacrifice, holy, acceptable to God, which is your reasonable service."* (Romans 12:1)

Presenting your body, or your life, past and present, to God is a holy, mature, or reasonable thing to do. Presenting yourself to God is the only thing *we* can do that is acceptable to God — because it is the only way, He can help us mature in Him.

The use of the word *altar* is, of course, a metaphor used to describe the process of offering something to God. Maybe *operating table* would be a better metaphor for today as we are literally presenting ourselves to God so He can do heart surgery on us. Replacing old lies with His truths. Issues that are keeping you from living a holy, peace-filled life can be very painful as you present them to God. That is why we have continued to run from them for as long as we have. However, trust God (Proverbs 3:5) as you present them to Him. He cares for you and can only speak peace to your issues as you patiently open yourself to Him.

Being afraid of your past is going to stop God from helping you grow into your future. We must become like the Apostle Paul and refuse to hang on to the past successes, thinking we have really done something. We must also let go of our past failures and tragedies believing we have committed such grievous errors that not even God can accept us.

This letting go occurs when we allow God to speak to our issues directly. We must press on to the future accomplishments in Christ. Issues or feelings that are keeping us from flowing with God and enjoying all He has for us are direct indicators that we need to experience Him — not run from Him. It is an indicator we need a little heart and soul surgery. Renewing the mind is receiving the truth that will make you free from the lies that are causing you the emotional pain.

"For the word of God is living and powerful, and sharper than any two-edged sword, piercing even to the division of soul and spirit, and of joints and marrow and is a discerner of the thoughts and intents of the heart" (Hebrews 4:12). The freshly spoken word from God is God's scalpel for heart and soul surgery.

"Let us therefore come boldly to the throne of grace that we may obtain mercy and find grace to help in time of need"

(Hebrews 4:16). This is God's operating room where He operates on our heart and soul.

Is your emotional pain causing you to behave in an unholy manner? Then it is time to remove the source, or change the root of the problem. If you are struggling with this thought, it might be good to return to the chapter on "renewing the mind" and study the scriptures presented there. Throughout this book, you will find additional examples of renewing the mind.

There is one last point I need to make here; *abstinence is not freedom.* Being able to abstain from your impulses is fine, but it is a far cry from what God has waiting for you.

Much of the time, our methods of abstaining are simply exchanging one form of bondage for another. For instance, I thank God for the work that Alcoholics Anonymous (AA) does with those trapped on alcohol and drugs. However, their freedom is not Jesus' promised freedom. Granted, their bondage is much less damaging than the affects and dangers of alcohol and drug addictions, but it still is not a freedom. Alcohol and drugs are methods of coping with emotional pain. Work-based plans of abstaining are just another coping method.

Jesus offers us total freedom. This means no desires or need to continue. No inner turmoil or hanging on, hoping you can make it. When the Lord set me free from alcohol, I had a full working bar in my family room and enough beer in our three refrigerators to float a small houseboat. I simply lost the desire to keep on drinking. I finally had to pour all that alcohol down the drain because it was just taking up space and I no longer needed it or wanted it. I was free enough that I could be around others that drank and it has never tempted me. That, my friend, is freedom.

We have worked with homosexuals who were working hard

abstaining from their sexual desires. One man came to us, no longer able to abstain and therefore, was caught in his sin. After his sin was exposed, he promised to seek help. He and his wife knew about us so he came to see if we could help him. A few minutes into the meeting, the Lord showed him a memory of himself as a little boy, around seven years old. That little boy suffered torment by being molested, and eventually sodomized by several older neighborhood bullies. This abuse went on for quite some time and the little boy had no one to whom he could cry out. He was so ashamed and humiliated he didn't want to tell his parents for fear of their possible response. Therefore, this little boy began to believe what the neighborhood boys called him, a fag and a queer.

Because of the trauma forced upon him, the constant name-calling he endured, and the inner torment he constantly battled, he believed the lie that he was homosexual and began to act out on a regular basis as he grew into manhood. He knew all along it was wrong (Romans 1:24-27), but because he believed a lie, he was unable to stop. He even married a lovely lady in order to feel normal and tried as hard as he could to abstain, thinking he was free. He did well fooling his new friends and coworkers, until the inner feelings took over, driving him into his sin and shame. The devil knows exactly how to tempt you when you least expect it and after you feel you have whipped it. From the moment the Lord spoke truth to his painful memories, this man has never again been tempted or driven into his old behavior.

Let's look for a moment, at what God has to say and what the *genuine* Christians believe about the current controversy of same-sex marriage and the movement to legitimize the homosexual lifestyle. However, remember the purpose of this book — to help those trapped find freedom. I am not against anybody or trying to find fault with any group. We will all give an account to God about our individual lifestyles (2Corinthians 5:10) and it certainly is not up to me to cast judgment. However, as the author, I do believe I have a responsibility to promote and teach the truth. Especially when I know that there are many out there desperately searching for understanding and help in finding inner peace. Therefore, the basis or foundation of truth to me is the Holy Bible. There is only one thing that upsets God and I do not wish to be a part of that — *suppressing the truth in unrighteousness* (Romans 1:18). Meaning to withhold the truth or cover the truth by another lie. Therefore, let us look at what the Book of Truth says about this subject with the rational, logical mind that God intends us to use as we search for His truths and plans for our lives.

First, the Bible says in Leviticus 18:22 and 20:13 that "for a man to lay with another man as with a woman and for a woman to lay with another woman as with a man, is an abomination." In Romans 1:24-27, "it is called uncleanness and a dishonoring of their bodies among themselves." It is called, "exchanging the truth of God for the lie, worshipping, and serving the creature rather than the Creator." It also says, "these are vile passions that go against nature which is shameful behavior." And finally, the Book of Revelation specifically states that, "the sexually immoral will be found outside the Holy City, cut off permanently from God, after the creation of the new heaven and new earth" (Revelation 22:14-15). Why would God be so against this lifestyle? This lifestyle goes against His natural order of things. God's natural order is for the purpose of procreation (Genesis 2:21-26, 6:19-20). Any practice that destroys or stops this is called unnatural, and in this case, as we just noticed, an abomination and unclean.

Mankind has blamed God for making mistakes and placing

women in men's bodies and men in women's bodies. If God makes mistakes like that in His very creation, then He is not perfect. If He is not perfect, He cannot be God. If God is imperfect then it really doesn't matter how we behave and everything in the Bible is a lie. I do not believe this for a second and I cannot believe any rational mind could believe it.

Man is accusing God of making people homosexual, as though it is the third sexual type of His creation. If this is true and I do not believe that it is, God is then an unjust tyrant — one who demands certain behavior but makes it impossible for some to follow His demands.

My final thought is this: If God is at fault that would naturally exonerate man from all wrongdoing. Natural man has been trying to blame God for man's failings since the very beginning (Genesis 3:12, 4:6-9). That is why we need a Savior and a Helper. In the natural, we will never be at peace with God or with ourselves. In the natural, we will never be free to enjoy all that life has to offer because we will never be at peace.

The promise is freedom to all who will communicate their pain to the Lord, not a method of abstaining, but honest, non-tempting freedom. We have had the pleasure of working with several trapped in the homosexual lifestyle. They stepped into it during their formative years, some by pressure and some voluntarily, but they all knew it wasn't normal. However, until they talked to the Lord, they were all miserable. Can you imagine trying to hide a secret like that? If you who are reading this currently live in this lifestyle and have a peace with yourself, I mean you no harm or embarrassment. I certainly do not judge you, which is neither my job nor my intent. However, many in the world today are confused about their sexual orientation and lifestyle. I deal with them almost daily. They are looking for answers and freedom. To them, I offer this input in the hopes they find their peace and their freedom.

This confusion and fear is going on within the church all the time and people are crying out for help. It is time to quit judging the fruit of their lives. It is time the body of Christ learns how to minister to these emotionally wounded people, helping them receive their freedom that Jesus paid for on the cross of Calvary.

Genuine Christians live a holy life by continuously allowing God to inspect their soul.

"Search me, O God, and know my heart; Try me, and know my anxieties; and see if there is any wicked way in me, and lead me in the way everlasting" (Psalm 139:23-24).

"Examine me, O Lord, and prove me; Try my mind and my heart. For your loving kindness is before my eyes, and I have walked in your truth" (Psalm 26:2, 3).

Do not be afraid of God's inspection. Be more afraid that you will escape His altar rather than fearing you will have to present yourself on it. We all have character flaws of one type or another. None of us has arrived and won't, until the Lord delivers us out of these flesh and blood bodies. There are many lies believed by all of us that make up our character flaws. Allowing God to locate them for us and showing us how they got there, is the only method of eliminating them.

I would rather have the freedom to work with God because I choose to, rather than have something I don't even know I have cause me problems when I least expect it. Take a look over the past twenty-five years at all the big ministries whose leaders fell due to some character weakness. If I were a betting man, I would bet that if they could do it all over again they would choose to work with God alone, at their own choosing, rather than falling to public disgrace, losing the way they did.

Do not waste your potential just because of some hard-to-deal-with issues you may have. If you are hiding anything, the devil will make it his business to make sure it gets exposed. Work with God willingly rather than allowing the devil to destroy you. There is hope and freedom awaiting you. It's your choice.

The Genuine Christian Understands the Love Walk

> *"Since you have purified your souls in obeying the truth through the Spirit in sincere love of the brethren, love one another fervently with a pure heart."* (1Peter 1:22)

Jesus said we would be known, or identified, as His disciples only as we love one another (John 13:34). Many have spent most, if not all, of their years as Christians trying to improve the quality of their love without first considering the HOW TO of loving the way Jesus loved us. When Jesus said "... *as I have loved you* ..." the majority of Christians take this to mean quality and quantity rather than *how I loved you*, or, the how to of being *agape* love. The quality and quantity of Jesus' love was unconditional and unrestrained. But, HOW did He love us this way is the thing we must learn, unless we are willing to settle for being less than *genuine*. If you do not understand exactly what *agape* love is, you end up making assumptions as you follow Jesus, finding yourself missing the mark much more often than you should. After all, Jesus did not give us a command to make us fail, so why are we failing at the most basic aspect of our Christian faith?

To see how we are failing you need only look at the squabbles in most churches, the failing marriages, stress-filled homes, and wayward children of Christian families to see something is missing. We have pretended to have the answer for the world without first taking care of our own lives and homes.

The love most Christians live is purely intellectual. Intellectual love means that cognitively, we know God said we must love others and we try to love others by sheer religious determination. This type of love is usually the product of a personal judgment and the resulting responses. This intellectual type of love is therefore, based upon how our judgments makes us feel. This is especially true when dealing with the unlovable characters of our society. Responding based upon how the person makes us feel is not the answer the world is waiting for. After all, this is the same behavior those without Christ exhibits. This is not what Jesus had in mind and it is not the product of the glorious church.

We do, however, have the answer the world is waiting for and will draw closer to becoming the glorious church as soon as we take care of a few spots and wrinkles. Once that takes place, we will begin to show the world the way and they will begin to ask us to show them because of what they see in us. Therefore, let's take care of a few spots and wrinkles in our own lives by examining carefully Jesus' command to *love one another, as I have loved you, that you also love one another.*

To begin with, let us look at the Greek definitions[7] to the key words in John 13:34. A *new command* I give you, Jesus said. The word translated *new* is from the Greek word *kainos*, number 2537 in Strong's. This word refers to qualitatively new, not new as in another command or numerically new. The command to *love one another* is not a numerically new command. Long before Jesus spoke these words to His disciples, He told the rich young ruler that the most important command was to *love the Lord with all your heart, mind and soul, and to love your neighbor as yourself, or in place of yourself.* (Matthew 22:37-40) This was Old Testament. Jesus was quoting Deuteronomy 6:5; 10:12; 30:6, and Leviticus 19:18. In John 13:34, Jesus is reminding His disciples about the old command and promising that He is going to help *improve our ability* or *give us His ability* to comply with the two most important commands ever given to mankind.

---

[7] All Greek or Hebrew word definitions are taken from; "The Hebrew-Greek Key Study Bible" Compiled and edited by Spiros Zodhiates, Th.D. AMG Publishers 1984.

This study bible utilizes Strong's Dictionary Vocabulary Helps numbering system.

The next word we will look at is the English word *love* from the Greek word *agapaō* meaning, *God's love toward man* and vice versa. *Agapaō* shares the same root with the word, *agapē* meaning *God's willful direction toward man.* Agape always gives what the one-loved needs not necessarily wants. Agape always gives what God wants for the recipient regardless of how it feels or what it costs. A good example of that is, *"God so loved the world that He gave ..."* not what the world wanted, but what the world needed, even at the cost of the very life of His only begotten Son.

Now, that being said, let's look at John 13:34 with this additional information in mind. Jesus said, "I am giving you a new ability to obey the command of love toward one another by making it possible for you to love *as I loved you.*" What Jesus did, we must do in order to accomplish what He accomplished. How else could God expect us to give to one another what He desires for that person? In our own strength alone, that is an impossible task.

Agape is giving to others what God desires them to have. We often try to *"be loving"* toward one another, rather than having God's love for one another. We have tried to *act out* 1Corinthians 13:1-8 by sheer determination and have failed. God's love is not an act, it is an *action.* Trying to act loving towards one another while harboring bitter feelings and pain inside does not work. Love is action driven by our compassion for one another. God can love through us in action as we process our painful issues with Him.

Our failure to do this has allowed the world's type of love, *Philio* or kindly affectionate friendship love (e.g. *you scratch my back and I will scratch yours.*) to enter the church, pushing agape out of the church. That is not God's plan. God did not give us His instructions to cause us to fail. So, why are so many failing?

God did not give us His instructions to cause us to work hard. So, why is the Christian community working so hard and accomplishing so little? We are working hard and failing because we do not fully understand the details of God's plan. Not understanding the *details* of the plan always causes failure and never allows us to reach our full potential with God. I fear that is where the average Christian is right now. We can, with a proper understanding of the Word, correct that. Let us be the generation that corrects it and gets it right.

What in the world, could God give us to make it possible to love this way? The answer takes us back to the opening scripture found in 1Peter. Let's look at 1Peter 1:22 in several different translations to begin to see something that may have eluded us to this point.

> *"Since you have purified your souls in obeying the truth through the Spirit in sincere love of the brethren, love one another fervently with a pure heart."* (NKJV)

> *"Now that you have cleaned up your lives by following the Truth, love one another as if your lives depended upon it."* (Message Translation)

> *"Now that you have purified yourselves by obeying the truth so that you have a sincere love for your brothers, love one another deeply, from the heart."* (NIV)

> *"Since you have in obedience to the Truth through the [Holy] Spirit you have purified your hearts for the sincere affection of the brethren, [see that you] love one another fervently from a pure heart."* (Amplified Version)

> *"Now that you have, by obeying the truth, made your souls clean enough for a genuine love of your fellows, see that you do love each other, fervently and from the heart."* (J.B. Phillips Translation)

I personally like the last translation the best. I think it speaks much clearer to what Peter is saying and follows perfectly what Jesus said in John 13:34. Until we get our soul purified or made clean enough, we will never have what the Bible calls a *genuine love of your fellows.* Many have stated to me, "I thought I was cleansed at the cross and by Jesus' blood." The Cross of Christ cleanses you from your own sin, but not from the pain inflicted by others. The soul is your mind and we must renew our mind with the truth. Your mind doesn't sin, but what is in it can drive you to sin. So what is a genuine love of your fellows? Let's find out, because herein lays the answer to successfully following Jesus.

As long as you have buttons (inner pain or issues) that people and situations in your life trigger, your soul is not *purified* or clean *enough* to have what the Bible calls a *genuine love* ***of*** *your fellows or* ***of*** *the brethren.* As long as others can control what you feel by their actions and words, your soul is impure. Jesus had no buttons because Jesus believed no lies. *"For the ruler of this world is coming, and he has nothing* ***in*** *Me"* (John 14:30).

Believing lies about oneself to be true is the cause of inner pain. Others cause that pain to come alive when they say or do something that pushes your buttons. Working with the Holy Spirit to purify your soul is allowing the Holy Spirit to locate your buttons and, with your help, disconnect them permanently by speaking truth to you. We must be obedient and responsive to the Holy Spirit, in order to purify our souls before we are able to allow His love to flow through us to others.

When God's love flows through a dirty vessel, it picks up the dirt, no longer remaining pure and powerful. A purified heart is a soul disinfected by the words spoken by the Holy Spirit.

The word in 1Peter 1:22 translated "soul" comes from the Greek word *psuchē*. Our soul, or psyche, is comprised of the following three parts: Our ***Intellect*** (all of your cognitive knowledge, reasoning, and thinking ability), ***Memory*** (pictures of experiences and their interpretations), and our ***Emotions*** (how you feel). These three parts determine what we believe and from that, we determine our will. Your will is what you choose to do with what you know and believe. Your will is also commonly referred to as your character. Our experiences and their interpretations form our beliefs. What we believe is the cause of our feelings. Our feelings drive our actions, developing our character.

A misinterpreted experience in life or a life of trauma causes us to believe lies about ourselves that need renewed with truth when our pain surfaces. Too many are running from the pains of life, blaming the devil or others for causing all their grief, never understanding that it is through the trials of life, and the pains they produce, that give God what He needs to purify their soul. James 1:2-4 calls it *"patience which yields maturity"* in our life. Soul purification or maturity occurs, as we take in the truth through study, as well as, through experiencing the truth by our communication with God during the experiences of life.

Loving others is not an intellectual thing. We cannot love others just because God says so. We love God because He first loved us. We love others because we love Him. We decide to love others because He gave His life for them. We are able to love others with God's love only when we have given the Holy Spirit total and complete use of our bodies. We love others as

He pours His love (words and actions) through us for them. Loving others is not an act of works or self-efforts but the result of trusting Jesus and following the Holy Spirit. Our very words must be His words (1Peter 4:11). Even our moments of silence must be the silence and peace we receive from Him, and our actions toward others must be in obedience to His immediate command. Loving others is not something we receive, but something we are allowing God to give others as He flows through us. Our love for others and the actions we take are a direct result of our relationship with the Lord. How we love others is therefore, the result of how we love God.

Without becoming a purified vessel through which the Holy Spirit can flow, you will continue failing as you measure your attitude, words and actions against 1Corinthians 13:4-8. However, as you allow the Holy Spirit to work *on* you and speak *to* you about *you* and your issues, you will begin to live in His perfect peace and rest. As you begin to live in His perfect peace and rest, it will become more natural to give the Holy Spirit total freedom to work through you and you will begin to expect Him to flow through you. The more comfortable we become abiding in Him the more confidence we gain, allowing others to sense a greater boldness coming from us. (Refer to Isaiah 32:17) You will then begin seeing the attributes of love being expressed in your life. Most importantly, others will witness His love through you long before you do, keeping you humble and pliable for the Lord. This is your witness for Him powered by the Holy Spirit that Jesus promised us in Acts 1:8.

I hope you can see that if you are having struggles being love in your horizontal relationships, your relationship with God is suffering as well. "*No one has seen God at any time. If we love one another, God abides in us, and His love has been perfected* (matured) *in us. By this* (By our physical actions of love for and words spoken to others.) *we know that we abide in Him, and He in us, because He has given us His Spirit."* (1John 4:12, 13 emphasis and comments added) This is where the horizontal relationships meet the vertical relationship revealing God in us through our attitudes, actions and our peace. The cross of Christ in our life bears witness to the reality of a <u>living</u> God of hope for all who will follow Him.

We can say we love God until we are blue in the face, but the only proof of it is when others can see that we are bold channels of living love from God toward others. This is also the only proof we have that we *abide in Him* and *He in us*. I have heard others say things like, "I just love Jesus with all my heart, but I am having a tough time with so-in-so." If you cannot love "so-in–so", the Word says, you cannot love God either.

> *"By this we know love, because He laid down His life for us. And we also ought to lay down our lives for the brethren. But whoever has this world's goods, and sees his brother in need, and shuts up his heart from him, how does the love of God abide in him? My little children let us not love in word or in tongue, but in deed and in truth. And by this we know that we are of the truth, and shall assure our hearts before Him" (1John 3:16-19). "If someone says, I love God, and hates his brother, he is a liar; for <u>he who does not love his brother whom he has seen, how can he love God whom he has not seen?</u> And this commandment we have from Him: that he who loves God <u>must</u> love his brother also."* (1John 4:20-21, emphasis added)

The commands we have to love the body of Christ and our neighbors apply double to our spouse! If we say we love God, we MUST love our spouse. That means, if we are following God, we cannot put them away or leave them without first seeking God in an attempt to reconcile. I fully understand that not every relationship is reconcilable but only God knows which ones are and are not. To make that decision without first hearing from God is rather presumptuous and is living by the flesh. Remember, this is about being *genuine* Christians!

If your relationship is physically or emotionally dangerous, a separation can be good as you seek help and help the offender find help. However, if your spouse will not seek help or refuses to cooperate with efforts to restore the relationship and live with you *as a Christian should*, you are free to protect yourself according to 1Corinthians 7:12-16. *"But to the rest I, not the lord, say: If any brother has a wife who does not believe, and she is willing to live with him, let him not divorce her. And a woman, who has a husband who does not believe, if he is willing to live with her, let her not divorce him. For the unbelieving husband is sanctified by the wife, and the unbelieving wife is sanctified by the husband, otherwise your children would be unclean, but now they are holy. But if the unbeliever departs, let him depart; a brother or a sister is not under bondage in such cases. But God has called us to peace. For how do you know, O wife, whether you will save your husband? Or how do you know, O husband, whether you will save your wife?"* The phrase I underlined "if he or she is willing to live with him or her", plus the phrase "God has called us to peace" is saying that to "live with a believer," the unbeliever must live with you in peace and within the guidelines of the Word of God. If they refuse to do that, you are no longer obligated to remain married. This is to protect the one abused, physically, emotionally or both. God would not force His children to live in danger. However, **I strongly suggest you seek Christian help before making any final decisions.** (Please notice I did not say "Christian opinions" but professional Christian help.)

Ignoring the situation and just quitting is not God's way. Jesus is a God of reconciliation (2Corinthians 5:18) and He has given us a ministry of reconciliation (2Corinthians 5:18) and the word of reconciliation (2Corinthians 5:19). How can we ever reconcile the world to God if we refuse to seek God's help and at least attempt to reconcile our own relationships?

If you are unable to be that channel of love to someone in your life, then you need to *look for the reason you* are unable, rather than blaming him or her. The *blame game* is a coping mechanism that says, "I'm OK. My pain is your fault." No one should be giving other people such power over their lives. If everyone in your life is responsible to make you happy, you are doomed to be miserable the rest of your life; causing spiritual maturity — becoming *genuine* as a Christian, to be an impossible dream. The answer to why you cannot love or be that channel of love to them is locked up in your soul, only to be discovered and dealt with as you allow the Holy Spirit to purify you (1Peter 1:22).

All interpersonal relationships will create, from time to time, uncomfortable, negative feelings. These feelings, generally, are not new to us. Neither are they necessarily born out of the actions and words exchanged in the relationship. Marriage relationships are even more capable of creating these bad feelings because you cannot run away from or hide from your spouse as you can from a more casual acquaintance. These feelings, created from life's experiences are stored in your soul (memory). Remember, lies believed to be true about you produce emotional pain. As we feel these negative feelings, we have two courses of action open to us: **1)** blame the other person for the feelings, or **2)** ask God where those feelings are coming from and then deal with them as God shows you. As He shows you their origin, tell Him what feels true about you *in that memory*.

Then listen quietly inside for a few seconds, giving God the time to speak truth to the lie that is causing your pain.

Why is it important to see the where and when (memory) of the occurrence? Because that is the origin, of the lie; where the wound occurred or the experience was misinterpreted. That is the *root* of the issue. Identifying the root memory or the *origin* of the lie, and receiving the truth from the Lord concerning that root memory seems to heal all other memories with similar wounds. However, looking at memories that are not the root, forces each memory to need addressing individually. Going directly to the root memory is the quickest way to receive permanent inner peace and rest.

When you ask Jesus to show you the root memory, trust Him with what He shows you. This is a great opportunity to exercise your faith. Only God knows the origin of the lie and He will show you when you ask Him. This is why psychological counseling does not heal. They are unable to find the root memory and change the lie with truth. This is because basic psychology does not believe, nor teach, that there is a God who desires to get involved with all of mankind's cares (1Peter 5:7) and fears (1John 4:18). Only our Creator, the Father of all living souls, can heal the soul of man.

Look with me at 1John 5:2 and 3. "By this we know that we love the children of God, when we love God and keep His commandments. For this is the love of God, that we keep His commandments. And His commandments are not burdensome."

If you are dealing with someone who is being difficult, it may seem like the commandments of God are burdensome unless you fully understand what John is trying to teach us here. The word translated as *commandments* comes from the Greek word *entolē*. The broader definition for *entolē* is: "a command, whether of God or man; an authoritative *prescription* or precept; an immediate command or directive." His commandments, referred to here, are not the *"thou shalt nots,"* but rather He is saying, "I have a word, a precept, a prescription for you that will change your life and help you (Hebrews 4:12). If you love me, you will listen to me and respond to me, so my love can flow through you to others."

If we listen to Him, He will give us the truth needed to take away the pain we feel and make it possible for us to respond in a Christ-like, or *genuine* manner. If we listen to Him, He will also guide our responses to others, as well as interpret each experience so we don't keep ingesting lies.

One day during a time of extended prayer, the Lord spoke something to me that I think might help you here.

"Walking in LOVE or abiding in Christ is as simple as focusing on me in all situations so that I can, 1) *Interpret the moment for you,* and 2) *Guide your responses.* When people and/or situations cause you to feel bad, I will have an immediate word for you which will bring Truth into the situation (a word of knowledge), causing you to be freed from the moment.

Many times the word I bring you will also give you your response or the appropriate action you must take (a word of wisdom), allowing my will to be worked through you.

Do not harden your heart to my voice (Hebrews 3:15). Hardening your heart is when you refuse to believe the thoughts that originated with me (They will always be positive. James 1:17-18), in favor of following the feeling of the moment, which is always negative. Entertaining or following the negative feelings of the moment is stepping out of me (Matthew 16:25) and living according to the flesh. Living this way always produces death (Matthew 16:26). Following the positive words I give is refusing the flesh (crucifying the flesh, Matthew

16:24) and that will always produce life." (Scriptures added for your edification.)

This is purifying the soul through the Spirit in sincere love of the brethren (1Peter 1:22a).

Jesus is truly alive in us by His Holy Spirit after we are born again (John 3:3). However, the only proof we are alive in, or abiding in Him, is by obeying His prescriptions He gives us throughout each day (1John 3:24). Unless we abide in Him, or listen and respond to Him, we will rarely if ever enter His rest, walk in His peace, love one another, or overcome the world (John 16:33). If we, through our life in Christ, do not overcome our world, we remain irrelevant, un-respond-able, and unnecessary to our culture and the people of our generation. What Jesus intended to be a powerful, supernatural relationship which emulates His life and deeds on the earth, ends up becoming a commonly ordinary, lifeless, religious exercise of futility.

A Genuine Christian Gives Up the Ways of the Flesh

> *"Therefore, laying aside all malice, all deceit, hypocrisy, envy and all evil speaking"* (1Peter 2:1)

The ways of the flesh are: getting even, protecting your turf, defending your honor, justifying the situation you find yourself in, blaming others for the physical situations of your life and for your inner pain, and working to perfect yourself, to mention a few. G*enuine* Christians allow God to defend, protect and perfect them, as well as deal with their inner pain and deliver them out of the tough places we all find ourselves in occasionally.

> *"For to this you were called, because Christ also suffered for us leaving us an example, that you should follow His steps: Who committed no sin, nor was deceit found in His mouth; who, when He was reviled, did not revile in return; when He suffered, He did not threaten, but committed Himself to Him who judges righteously."* (1Peter 2:21-23, empha-

sis added)

This is a true mark of a *genuine* Christian. One who trusts God to defend his honor, and his name. After all, we now have a new name and God is responsible and has promised to defend it for us. We also have a new purpose and God has promised to smooth out the rough paths and pull us through the tough places as we trust Him. His greatest desire is to perfect, or mature us in His love and nature. This occurs as we trust Him to take us through the tough places in life, dealing with the painful feelings that will surface.

Sometimes it seems that everything in life is a struggle. It seems like we are the only ones who have to give in, say I'm sorry, turn the other cheek, or offer forgiveness. Well, in fact, we are. We have something supernatural going on inside us and for us that the world knows nothing about. We have the supernatural ability to turn the other cheek and to trust God to protect and mature us while the world looks on in amazement. In fact, it is good they are looking on so they can see us in action. This is being a witness for Christ (Acts 1:8). In fact, *genuine* Christians are more concerned with their life being a witness daily, than they are about going out occasionally to witness. If they see us going through enough, always coming out unscathed when life drops its bombs on us, they might just ask us to explain it (1Peter 3:15). That should be what we are living for, not hoping we escape all the pressures and trials. There is no profit in escaping or running from the issues and conflicts of life.

The Apostle Paul knew what suffering for his faith was all about. Look at what he said in Romans 8:18, 19:

"For I consider that the sufferings of this present time are

> *not worthy to be compared with the glory which shall be revealed in us. For the earnest expectation of the creation eagerly waits for the revealing of the sons of God."* (Romans 8:18, 19, emphasis added)

I am concerned that many people think that the "*glory to be revealed in us*" that Paul was talking about, will only come after we are in heaven. That is not what the Apostle Paul is telling us. We don't need the glory of God on us in heaven, for we will be living in the glory of God there. We need the glory of God on us and revealed in us here on the earth where the people of the world, the non-believers, are watching. Remember what verse 19 says? They are eagerly waiting for the revealing of the sons of God. Who are the sons of God? They are *genuine* Christians, just normal people like you and I, who decide to be led by the Holy Spirit. They are people, like us, who understand the value of the trials we all face and are patiently working with God to overcome, reflecting His glory in their life.

Controlling the Thoughts of the Mind

When considering the topic of giving up the ways of the flesh, we have a tendency to overlook the activity of the mind. Your mind, if not trained and controlled, can become your enemy. Your mind wants control and it will never lead you in the ways of God.

> *"Because the carnal [fleshly] mind is enmity against God; for it is not subject to the law of God, nor indeed can be."* (Romans 8:7, comment added)

Your mind, in the context of verse 7, is not referring to your intellect or your memory. Verse 7 is not referring to the thoughts of the mind; verses 5 and 6 already took care of that.

> *"For those who live according to the flesh set their minds on the things of the flesh, but those who live according to the Spirit, the things of the Spirit. For to be carnally minded* [fleshly thoughts] *is death, but to be spiritually minded* [spiritual thoughts] *is life and peace."* (Romans 8:5

and 6, comments and emphasis added for clarity)

Verse 7 is telling us that because our mind is flesh, we must be on guard and recognize that this organ called the mind, or the brain, will work against God, as does the basic nature of all flesh. Your flesh always protects and perfects itself. Therefore, it becomes very important to build yourself up spiritually so you can control the flesh, which, of course, includes your brain.

Your brain is a powerful "shoulder-top" computer with multitasking capabilities. One task is to serve as an electrical control unit for the physical body's motor skills, as well as to monitor and control the rhythm of the heart. The spirit man uses and controls the other functions for thinking, identifying, memory storage and recall. If your mind, or brain, works against God, it is automatically working against you as a child of God. Therefore, as a Christian you must take control of the thoughts of your mind. Your mind does not define you as a person. To illustrate that point, I want you to lay the book down for a second and point to yourself — that's right, point to you, then pick the book up, and continue because I have a purpose here.

Come on, you have to work with me here — point to yourself. Thank you. Now, if you are like most people I have asked to do this, you pointed to your chest or your belly area, proving that it is *not* your mind that defines you as a person — it is your spirit. We are human spirits living in physical flesh and we possess a soul.

What do I mean by *defines* you? Your spirit does not reside in your mind — the soul does. Your spirit resides within your body cavity and uses your mind's capacity of thought, memory, and recall. Your mind is a tool to help you, not to set your value or purpose by guiding you. When you are led by your brain — your shoulder-top computer, allowing your mind to run away with its own thoughts, it is defining you. You are giving your shoulder-top computer the upper hand in your life. Whatever your brain tells you that you are you believe you are. Whatever your brain assumes you cannot do, you believe it and quit trying or never try at all. That is what I mean by "defining your value". That is why one points to one's body rather than one's head when pointing to self. With that understanding, let's move on and look at how to take control of our mind and begin defining ourselves by who we really are and by what God has created us to become.

It all starts with taking captive every thought. Taking captive every thought, becomes natural when you understand what God means when He instructs us to *bring every thought captive to the obedience of Christ.*

> *"For though we walk in the flesh, we do not war according to the flesh. For the weapons of our warfare are not carnal but mighty in God for pulling down strongholds, casting down arguments and every high thing that exalts itself against the knowledge of God, bringing every thought into captivity to the obedience of Christ, and being ready to punish all disobedience when your obedience is fulfilled."* (2Corinthians 10:3-6, emphasis added)

Let's start with the first underlined section *"... pulling down strongholds,"* and identify what a stronghold is. I have always defined a stronghold as the excuses we give ourselves to stay the way we are, the mental reasoning we use to excuse ourselves. Many times our immediate response to a problem is, "It's not my fault, so-in-so made me do it, or so-in-so made me feel this way!" When we refuse to look at ourselves honestly, looking for someone else to blame for our problems and difficulties, we are in the process of building and fortifying our strongholds. Strongholds are coping mechanisms that we use to stay the way we are. Coping mechanisms, or the fight to stay the way we are, is spiritual apathy. Spiritual apathy is the process of spiritual death — not a good place to be if you desire to become *genuine.*

God's Word says we have weapons that are mighty *in God* to pull down our strongholds. As we are born again, the Holy Spirit becomes incarnate or infused in our spirit. He will do what we cannot when we work with Him. God actually does the work, as reported in the book of Philippians.

> *"For it is God who works in you both to will and to do for His good pleasure."* (Philippians 2:13)

In this case, we must allow Him to destroy our excuses. The difficult part is seeing ourselves as we are and then being honest enough with ourselves to admit we have some strongholds to demolish. If you cannot admit you have strongholds, God is unable to help you any further with this mind battle. However, if you can understand that God is on your side and is working to set you free from all the junk that holds you back, admitting you have strongholds is actually the first step to victory. Once you admit it, it's gone.

The second underlined section is *"casting down arguments".* Here is where you begin to control the thoughts of your mind because the arguments the Word is referring to are the arguments we have with ourselves. Along with casting down arguments, we are to cast down every *"high thing"* that sets itself against or above the knowledge of God.

When you have thoughts like, "I can't do that, it's too hard," you have a *high thing* that just set itself above the scripture, *"I can do all things through Christ who strengthens me"* (Philippians 4:13).

The arguments we have with ourselves are always self-defeating, self-condemning, or self-exalting. Inner arguments are the enemy's plan to keep you out of the blessings of God. Inner arguments are always *high things* that set themselves above or against what God has already told us.

This is one more reason why a good working knowledge of the written Word of God is necessary — so the child of God can fight the good fight of faith and live in the victory and freedom Jesus paid for. Without an understanding of what God thinks of you, you will never be able to live in His victory. If you do not understand what God thinks of you and know what He has told us about His help in time of need, you will have a strong tendency to give up. Without an understanding of the written Word of God, you will be more likely to give in to fear. The Word of God will help you understand that there is more going for you than against you. Plus, the Word of God feeds your spirit, giving you the strength and maturity necessary to fight against the power of the brain's thoughts and life's circumstances.

Sometimes circumstances can become overwhelming regardless of your maturity and knowledge level. Therefore, your communication with the Lord becomes more important than ever. If you tell the Lord what you are feeling or thinking, He will speak to your circumstances and help you get through them. Speak to the Lord. This is something I tell Christians all the time and many look at me as if I am from a different planet or something. They say, "Out loud?" Or, "You mean just speak what I am feeling to God?" That is just what I mean.

Just speak to God about what you are feeling. [8] Chances are, you will be telling someone close to you what you feel or don't feel anyway. The only problem with telling people is they cannot help you much. When you tell God, you open the door to allow Him to help you. You are inviting Him into your circumstances. When you invite Him into your circumstances, you are taking advantage of the weapons of our warfare, which are mighty in God.

For many years, as a pastor, I would offer those I counseled exactly what I believe God was telling me about their situation. Some would receive and change but many would say they understood and go away none the better. When you offer others advice or counsel, the person listening is, more than likely, hearing it with the cognitive or intellectual part of their brain. To affect change and healing, they need to affect their experiential memory. When you help someone hurting talk to God about what *feels true to them,* they are in their experiential memory and therefore will receive permanent change as their *experiential* memory becomes renewed.

To understand what it means to bring every thought into captivity to the obedience of Christ, let's look at the Greek

---

[8] For a more complete understanding of why we must speak audibly to God, please refer to Appendix I entitled, *Why Must We Speak Audibly To God?*

word that was translated *obedience.* The Greek word is *hupakoē,* number 5218 in Strong's. The meaning given by Strong's is as follows; "to obey, listen to something, hearken, give heed to, follow or yield. Like a servant, soldier or a pupil." With this definition of *hupakoē,* or its English translation *obedience,* we have a little better chance of more fully understanding how to bring every thought into the obedience of Christ. Let's read 2Corinthians 10:5 with this expanded understanding.

> *"Casting down arguments and every high thing that exalts itself against the knowledge of God, bringing every thought into captivity by listening, hearkening, giving heed to and obeying Christ as His servant, soldier or pupil."*

As thoughts begin to lead us away from God by belittling, condemning, or overly exalting us, we need only say, "No. I'm not allowing you to do that to me!" and then listen, hearken, give heed to follow or yield to Christ as His servant, soldier, or a good pupil would. After we have received from the Lord and obeyed the word He spoke concerning the battle, the Lord will then be able to punish all disobedience from any spiritual or physical situations or entities that brought the thoughts to you in the first place.

Anytime we are in a mental battle with self-condemning or self-exalting thoughts, the Lord will come to our rescue with His word on the subject. As you call on Him, you are stripping the mind of the power to push you around. Make your mind serve you by directing it to work on the subjects about which you desire to think. If you need some inner peace, then tell your mind to be still in Jesus' Name. Quit allowing your mind to be in control of your destiny. Have you noticed that your mind can get you into more trouble than it has the ability to figure out? That alone would be a good reason to quit following it around and begin to take control once again.

We have helped people defeat depression with an understanding of how to control the thoughts of their minds. Philippians 4:8 is another scripture that is very helpful when it comes to controlling your thoughts.

> *"Finally brethren, whatever things are true, whatever things are noble, whatever things are just, whatever things are pure, whatever things are lovely, whatever things are of good report, if there is any virtue and if there is anything praiseworthy—meditate on these things."* (Philippians 4:8, emphasis added)

Do not let your mind bring you into depression by bringing bad news to you or taking you into an old experience that is now history. Your mind will replay the old battles of your life repeatedly and with each time through, your condition, within your mind, will get worse. Therefore, tell your mind to hush up and then put this scripture to work by forcing it to think about something *true, noble, just, pure, lovely, good news, or of anything with virtue or a praiseworthy value.* If what your mind is thinking about does not pass this test then tell your mind to hush. Speak to your mind and say, "In Jesus' Name, I command you to be quiet. I do not want you to speak to me about anything unless the Holy Spirit speaks to me. In Jesus' Name, Be still." Train your mind to work for you; quit working for your mind. Make your computer work for you. Quit working for your computer.

As you build your relationship with the Lord, by studying His Word and communicating with Him about your issues, your confidence level in Him will increase as your spirit man grows to maturity. In fact, if you don't build your relationship with the Lord, your confidence level in Him will not grow at all. If you don't take the opportunity to work with God on the daily, smaller issues, what makes you think you will trust Him for the big things to come?

Your spirit man and the Holy Spirit define who you are and what you have the capacity to become in life. Your flesh will constantly work against you making you think and feel that you are less than God has designed you to become.

Therefore, who or what are you going to listen to and follow. Follow the voice of God and His Word to constant victory or follow your fleshly thoughts and feelings to self-destruction. The choice is yours — it's time to do the responsible thing and become *genuine.*

Exercising Your Authority

Understanding your authority as a Christian is very important to understand when concerned with giving up the ways of the flesh. Over the years, we have ministered to many Christians whose lives were in a tailspin. Many of them were seemingly doing all the right things, but victory continued to elude them. As we worked with them it became obvious that they knew little to nothing about their spiritual authority, what it meant, and how to use it.

Enemies constantly surround us. As I just mentioned, your mind can work against you, becoming your enemy. The world system and its ideologies and beliefs are against God, making our very environment our enemy. Also, there is the unseen dark spiritual world of the demonic that is our enemy. In fact, everything in our life that works against God's plan for our freedom, peace and our spiritual success is our enemy.

Boy, that's painting with a broad brush, now isn't it. Well, let's narrow it just a bit to understand how to stand against *everything* that stands against us. Look with me at Luke 10:19 for a minute.

> *"Behold, I give you the* ***authority*** *to trample on serpents and scorpions, and over all the power of the enemy, and nothing shall by any means hurt you."*

I underlined the word *authority* for helping you understand that God is on our side. He said that with this authority we can trample on the enemy. Snakes and scorpions are symbolic for the forces of darkness that work against God's kingdom all the time. In fact, He said something quite startling we need to pay attention to when it comes to understanding and exercising our authority. He said that *nothing* shall by any means hurt or harm us. It is God's plan to keep us in His perfect peace and rest. If something is harming, alarming, or causing us inner turmoil, then we obviously are not exercising our authority. Now, please note this. It did not say that we would never have problems. It said that when problems strike, we have the authority to stand against them so that they cannot permanently harm us. It is even God's plan that future problems do not take us by surprise (John 16:13).

Let's talk a bit about how we use this authority against the enemy. First, you must recognize that you and I are human spirits living in flesh, blood, and bone bodies. We have already discussed the fact that our minds do not define us and neither do our bodies. Our bodies and our minds are tools given to us by the Lord so we can accomplish something on this earth. Because we are spirit beings and God is Spirit (John 4:24), Luke 10:19 is referring to the authority we have in the spiritual realm. You cannot walk into the grocery store and use your authority to acquire groceries, unless you physically own the store.

However, spiritually speaking, the kingdom of God is within us. Therefore, any attempts to stop God and the growth of His kingdom will come against us. Righteousness, peace, and joy in the Holy Spirit are ours to enjoy as we live in and advance the kingdom of God (Romans 14:17).

This kingdom cannot be shaken (Hebrews 12:28), but there will be many who try to shake it by messing with you. This pressure from the worldly continues while God continues shaking the heavens and the earth (Hebrews 12:25-27) as well. There is a whole lot of shaking going on and it is normal for there to be things within you that need removed. This is as it should be. We all have things in us that we need to get rid of. Most of the time we will never even know that stuff is in us until the pressure is on and the shaking begins. The Kingdom of God is only advanced, however, as aggressive sons of God *(genuine Christians)* hang in there through the tough times, listening to God, and exercising their God-given authority over the enemy (Matthew 11:12).

Genuine Christians recognize that life is not a Sunday school picnic. Life is an adventure that has good guys, bad guys, and heroes in it. Our adventure has two kings ruling two kingdoms. One kingdom is the Kingdom of Light and the other is the kingdom of darkness. The kingdom of darkness is constantly warring against the Kingdom of Light and all its subjects. Even our bodies at times plot against us and work with the kingdom of darkness to destroy us. The very ground on which we walk is controlled by the kingdom of darkness for now.

Our King has a Son that is working to make sure that everyone everywhere understands that His Father loves them all and has a plan to rescue them. The war rages daily. We must wise up and realize as soon as we awake each morning, that today an enemy will try his best to destroy us or slow us down. Our mission, since we have chosen to accept it, is to work with the King's Son and the King's chief Servant (Holy Spirit) to advance the Kingdom of Light every day.

Our King's Son has provided us everything we need to keep the enemy from harming us, but if we don't use it, we will get hurt and possibly even cut off from the Kingdom of Light. According to Jesus, we have the keys to the Kingdom. One set of keys is for *binding* our enemy and his actions against us.

> *"And I will give you the keys of the kingdom of heaven, and whatever you bind on earth will be bound in heaven, and whatever you loose on earth will be loosed in heaven."* (Matthew 16:19)

If *confusion* attacks and you do nothing about it, *confusion* is going to harm you. However, you can *bind confusion* from operating against you because of the authority you have been given. If some unseen force is attacking your family, your children are becoming unruly, and you do nothing about it, guess what will happen. You and your family will suffer harm by the attack. If you do nothing you will lose. If you choose to stand up and use the authority you have, you can ward off any attack and trample on the enemy every time.

The Lord (our King's Son) has also provided us with personalized armor and has given us instructions on its use. However, if we choose not to put it on (daily) you will be hurt and possibly cut off. Remember, this is no Sunday school picnic. This is war and our enemy is out to kill, steal, and destroy (John 10:10). Let's read the instructions given us concerning our armor.

> *"Therefore take up the whole armor of God that you may be able to withstand in the evil day, and having done all, to stand. Stand therefore having girded your waist with truth,*

> *having put on the breastplate of righteousness, and having shod your feet with the preparation of the gospel of peace; Above all, taking the shield of faith with which you will be able to quench all the fiery darts of the wicked one. And take the helmet of salvation and the sword of the Spirit, which is the word of God."* (Ephesians 6:13-17)

You have the authority to use this armor.

> *"Put on the whole armor of God that you may be able to stand against the wiles of the devil."* (Ephesians 6:11)

If you are smart, daily you will consider yourself a target for the enemy's fiery darts. That is why He says to put on the armor. You are taking your spiritual life in your own hands if you don't daily remind the enemy that you are wearing God's armor.

The Lord has given us the authority to use His blood. The enemy cannot cross the bloodline (Exodus 12:13). That is why the blood is a part of the *genuine* Christians daily prayer. I apply the blood to my family, ministry, and myself daily. If you never use the blood, you are an easy target for the enemy.

> *"And they overcame him [our enemy] by the blood of the Lamb and the word of their testimony."* (Revelations 12:11a, comment added)

We must apply the blood to enjoy the victory Jesus purchased for us. *Genuine* Christians remain under the blood where they are kept safe (Exodus 12:13). To apply the blood means we stand our ground and notify the enemy verbally that our loved ones and we are under the Blood of Jesus because of our faith in Him and His work on the cross. It is a verbal declaration of our position in Him. It is our testimony that Jesus paid for us and washed us clean by His Blood. Under the Old Covenant, actual blood from a spotless animal was literally applied, or sprinkled, on the people and their homes. Under the New Covenant, we apply it by our declaration of faith in Jesus' work on the cross (Matthew 12:34b, 37).

There is one more tool the Lord has given us authority to use — the Name. We have the authority to use His Name.

> *"And whatever you ask in My Name, that I will do, that the Father may be glorified in the Son. If you ask anything in My name, I will do it."* (John 14:13, 14, emphasis added)

There is no other name given to man whereby others might be saved (Acts 4:12). That name is far above all powers and principalities and at the mere mention of that name knees will bow in heaven, on earth and under the earth (Philippians 2:9, 10). It is your choice to use His Name or to ignore it. If you do not use it, you will be hurt before this war is over. To use His Name is, once again, to stand firm by declaring verbally that the Name of Jesus is the authority within which we operate. To operate under or within the authority of Jesus' Name means that when we speak to God the Father, He receives our communication as though it was from Jesus Himself.

Now, let's look at how to use all this gear and how to appropriate His authority to work for us. Here is a sample prayer that will utilize everything we have just mentioned. This is not the only prayer that will work of course. However, it is an example of how you identify and use your authority to keep the enemy at bay or to foil his attack against you.

"Father, I thank you for the armor you have provided me so I can stand against the enemy's plan for me today. I put on the helmet of salvation to protect the mind of Christ; I put on the breastplate of righteousness because I am the righteousness of God through my faith in Jesus Christ. I now gird everything together with the belt of truth. Truth is my motivator. All lies in my life must yield to the Truth. The enemy king is the father of all lies but I bow to the Father of all Truth — Jesus my Lord. I run from the voice of the enemy. I shod my feet with my preparation in the Gospel of peace so that I may be able to move swiftly when called upon or stand firm and sure-footed during a direct attack. I pick up the shield of faith with which I put out all the flaming arrows of the enemy and skillfully wield the Spirit's sword, the Word of God. The Spirit's sword has the ability to stop the enemy cold and discern the very thoughts and intents of my own heart. I choose to have my heart changed where needed in order to line up with God's perfect plan for me.

"In the Name of Jesus, I take my authority you have provided me in Luke 10:19 and stand against the enemy's plan to defeat me.

"Enemy, I bind you and your workers who have been assigned to defeat me. I declare you cannot operate against me in Jesus' Name. I loose you from duty against me in Jesus' Name. I plead the Blood of Jesus over my family, my ministry and all those who will come to us for help.

"Satan, I command you, your underlings and workers in Jesus' Name, to keep your hands off those whom God is sending to us for help. You cannot touch them or harm them, because of the blood of Jesus.

"Jesus, thank you for victory and for all that you are accomplishing in me and through me for the Kingdom today.

Amen."

Genuine Christians understand their authority, how to use their protective armor and weapons for the advancement of the Kingdom of God.

Additionally, our natural flesh wants to seek its own justice; this is also known as getting even. Because many misunderstand forgiveness, it's important to know how to properly deal with our anger. Understanding how to deal with your anger will help you gain a proper appreciation and understanding of forgiveness and justice.

Genuine Christians Properly Deal with Their Anger

> *"Be angry and do not sin: Do not let the sun go down on your wrath."* (Ephesians 4:26)

There are many people who have a difficult time dealing with anger. Some think anger is sin and therefore hate to admit that they are angry. I hope you can see from the opening scripture in Ephesians that anger is not sin. However, what you do with it and how you choose to respond in your anger can be sin.

If you allow yourself, or are triggered, into a rage expressing your wrath physically and verbally in a destructive way, your response would be considered sin.

Likewise, if you hold on to your anger without expressing it, but mentally store the feelings in the back room of your mind, this response could be considered sin as well. People who do this generally call their anger "hurt feelings," and usually have a difficult time dealing with the people, the situations and the feelings, causing their anger.

Unfortunately, storing these feelings is personally taking on the offense, making it impossible to obey the command of love which ultimately causes your faith to fail (Galatians 5:6). Offense (internalized anger) causes people to reject each other, splits churches, families, and friends, and even causes many to walk away from their God-given call and ultimately, like Esau, their inheritance (Hebrews 12:15-17, Genesis 25:33).

People who internalize their anger will eventually explode in a fit of rage when they can no longer carry any more. They misinterpret this explosion as their anger. This, however, is actually the *wrath* of their anger. This explosion is caused by internalizing days, weeks, months, or even years of anger erroneously defined as "hurt feelings". Internalizing anger is like filling a pressure tank with an air pump. Once the tank has reached its capacity and the pump continues to pump, a dangerous explosion is unavoidable.

Anger is a secondary emotion that comes to protect us from emotions that feel worse than the anger. Anger therefore is the fruit of all inner turmoil including most *fear*. That is why Jesus said; *"Let <u>not</u> your heart be troubled, neither let it be <u>afraid</u>"* (John 14:27b).

Fear comes when we feel we are about to lose something, or to be exposed, found defenseless and/or out of control. In my own life, I suffered from feelings of inadequacy. When these feelings surfaced, I became angry and externalized my anger through rage. Anger and rage were the *fruit* of my life, while feelings of inadequacy, and the memories that produced them, were the *root* cause. By ignoring or internalizing the anger, I would have never gotten free of the feelings of inadequacy. However, venting my anger through rage was a very destructive and sinful way to live; none the less, it did drive me to seek more help than hiding it would have.

Internalized anger is equally destructive as well because it allows bitterness and revengeful feelings to control you. *"And his master was angry, and delivered him to the torturers until he should pay all that was due to him"* (Matthew 18:34). I believe these feelings are much of what this scripture is referring to when it speaks of the *torturers.* The torturers can also be demonic activity given access to your mind by the anger and bitterness.

You may have a difficult time believing that a Christian can be a host to demonic activity, but they can. These evil spirits reside in the lies of the mind. During our years of helping hundreds of people resolve their anger and being released from their emotional pain, we have seen many cases of demonic activity while dealing with unresolved anger.

Please be cautious not to deny the existence of something you have had no experience with. This could cause you to be a target in the future. Always remain teachable and ready to receive new revelation from the Lord, and you will mature much quicker. Always test the spirit of things by asking the Lord to verify or reject them for you. By staying in communication with the Lord, you will be kept safe.

The main point is, you cannot walk in the perfect peace the Lord Jesus provided for us (John 14:27) if you have unresolved anger dwelling in you. You will be constantly tormented by those who have hurt and offended you because, as those memories and their associated feelings are triggered, the offenders continue to drive your responses and thoughts, thereby taking control of your life.

For many people who have been terribly injured through repeated abuse (physical or mental), offering forgiveness to those who have sinned against them is a hard concept to grasp. I think one reason for this is because we have done a poor or weak job of teaching the principles of forgiveness. Allow me to make a few simple but scripturally sound comments concerning what forgiveness is and is not before we continue.

Forgiveness is not—

1. denial you suffered an injustice.
2. silence about the injustice you suffered.
3. denial of righteous anger.
4. denial of your desire for and right to justice.
5. a *get out of jail free card* for those who have sinned against you.
6. the act of reconciliation. However, it makes reconciliation possible.
7. Forgiveness does not weaken your defense against the same thing happening again in the future.

Forgiveness is—

1. trusting God.
2. releasing the pain caused by the offense thereby freeing the one offended from the control of the offender.
3. willingness, on the part of the one offended, to release the offender to God (John 20:23) so God can deal with the one who hurt them thereby getting them their deserved justice, as well as work to protect them, from any future occurrences.

Experience has taught us that the pain of anger and bitterness keeps the one who offended you in control of your life until you release them as instructed in Matthew 18:34-35. This pain and control are the *torturers,* or in some translations the *jailers.* The English word *forgiveness* comes from the same word translated *divorce.* Divorce means to *send away.* Forgiveness is therefore *sending the offense and offender away.* As we forgive, we *release* the offender and the offence *to God.*

While discussing this very topic and the best way to word it with a dear friend of mine, he told me of his experience in business when he and his wife were taken advantage of and how they finally got free of the torment of their experience. I hope his experience helps you understand more fully what I am trying to teach you as he recounts his experience in gaining

Freedom from the Torturers

John 20:23:

> *If you forgive the sins of any, they are forgiven them; if you retain the sins of any, they are retained.* (NKJV)
>
> *If you forgive someone's sins, they're gone for good. If you don't forgive sins, what are you going to do with them?* (Message)

"I started a business in a small town together with my wife and we had personally managed and operated this business, building it up into a community known and well-liked service business. Our reputation was excellent in the community and our bookings would run sometimes six weeks in advance to get an appointment. While managing the first business we saw the need to build a better machine to help us so we began a manufacturing business selling machines to similar service industry businesses. We began to sell equipment so fast that we could no longer manage both businesses, and as a result decided to sell the first business.

"We had a young couple working for us at the time that we felt needed a break and we wanted to help them get started. My wife and I both agreed to sell them our reputable service business for a minimal amount down and we would carry the rest on a private contract. We had the contract drawn up and both parties signed with everyone in agreement. This happily went on for a few months until the new owners stopped making their payments. We tried to be helpful and understanding about giving them an opportunity to catch up; however, they were making no effort to do so. We finally had to draw up a legal letter requesting they pay up in order to avoid legal channels of collection. Much to our surprise, we received a letter in the mail from their attorney that they were suing us for breach of the contract. This included some twisted allegations, an altered D.O.T. map, and a false charge concerning the non-compete clause of the contract. We were mortified that this couple, whom we had trusted so completely, could even entertain the thought of suing us, especially after carrying their contract and helping set them up in a business that was making more money at the time than even our new business.

"The result of all this was that anger began to rise up in my wife and me. We endured five years of legal litigation, depositions, and attorney fees all the while knowing that this couple didn't have to make a single business payment as long as they could stay out of court. To make things even harder, when we would see them in public they would vocally curse at us using obscenity and four-letter words, calling us names and making gestures not fit to talk about here or anywhere else. One evening in the middle of the night my wife couldn't sleep, she was sitting in the living room about 3:00 in the morning when a car pulled up in front of our house. She got me out of bed just in time to see the man who was suing us, get out of his car and throw a quart beer bottle through the front windshield of our pickup. That set us both right over the edge, consumed with anger for this couple we called the police and tried to report this matter. The police said there was nothing they could do about it. I was so angry I was ready to fist fight if given the opportunity.

"Then, one day I was driving my car down the main highway in town and I heard the Lord speak to me. He said that I needed to forgive them for what they had done and to give up my anger. I was upset even at the thought of letting my anger go because I felt like I was letting them off the hook for what they had done to us. When I expressed this to God, He said to me, *"If you refuse to forgive them and don't give up your anger I will have to let you deal with them, but if you forgive and release your anger and trust me, I will deal with them."* I didn't know what to say! I thought about what God had said for a few days and even talked with my wife about it.

"After several days of contemplation, I decided God would be better at dealing with them than I would so I had a meeting with God and audibly forgave and gave God all my anger. I felt so much better instantly, and I even began to feel sorry for them, for God was showing me glimpses of how miserable they were spiritually. My wife, on the other hand, didn't have as easy a time of forgiving as I did, but eventually within the course of few weeks, she also let go through forgiveness, and received peace. To make a long story short, the man who sued us for the business he never paid for got caught molesting a teenager, lost his reputation, and through drug abuse, lost the business. In time, he lost his wife and left town like a whipped pup. We opened the business with a name change and in a few months gained most of our old business back again. Now, it is no coincidence that while we maintained our anger and refused to forgive, the suing party was out buying new cars, dressed in the best clothes, enjoying life to the fullest and not giving us a thought, other than trying to get us for all they could. Neither do I believe that it is a coincidence, that as soon as we released our anger and forgave them, their lives began to fall apart for the recompense of their reward. It wasn't that we were happy over their loss. Quite the contrary, we found ourselves praying for their good, asking God to help them.

"The lesson God taught me in all this is that I was holding back justice by retaining their sin through anger and not forgiving, or releasing them. In essence, I was trying to take God's place in this situation. When I relinquished my attempt to deal with the situation and trusted God to do it, I remitted, or sent back on them, the sin and left the responsibility in the hands of God, the only one who could really do anything about it anyway. I don't think God was trying to hurt them but in his mercy allowed their own sin to find them out. I also believe God was trying to help them come to repentance, whether they did or not I don't know for I have lost track of them for many years but the lesson I learned here I will never forget. The time God taught me and my wife about the ins and outs of forgiveness."

According to John 20:23, we can bind the offender to the offense and hold them if we choose. However, when this is done, God is unable to deal with the sin of the one who hurt you. You have taken the place of God when you do not forgive, or release, the offender to God. God cannot seek justice for you until you are willing to release the event and the offender to Him.

> *"If you forgive [divorce or send away] the sins of any, they are forgiven them [sent away]; if you retain [bind or hold on to] the sins of any, they are retained."* (John 20:23, comments added)

Releasing the offender by offering them forgiveness has nothing to do with the offender's guilt or innocence. It is up to God, our Righteous Judge, to determine that (Romans 12:19). Those offended or sinned against are responsible to release the offender and his sin to God so God can acquire justice and freedom for the one offended.

Here are two more, out of many, scriptures that deal with the need to forgive those who have offended or hurt us in life.

> *"Then Peter came to Him and said, "Lord, how often shall my brother sin against me, and I forgive him? Up to seven times?" Jesus said to him, "I do not say to you, up to seven times, but up to seventy times seven."…"Then his master, after he had called him, said to him, 'You wicked servant! I forgave you all that debt because you begged me. Should you not also have had compassion on your fellow servant, just as I had pity on you? And his master was angry, and delivered him to the torturers until he should pay all that was due to him. So My heavenly Father also will do to you if each of you, <u>from</u> <u>his</u> <u>heart</u>, does not forgive his brother his trespasses."* (Matthew 18:21-22, 32-35, emphasis added)

> *"And whenever you stand praying, if you have anything against anyone, forgive him that your Father in heaven may also forgive you your trespasses. But if you do not forgive, neither will your Father in heaven forgive your trespasses"* (Mark 11:25-26)

When seeking the perfect inner peace offered by Jesus (John 14:27), it is very important to deal with anger in the proper way. I have found that when it is impossible to obtain inner healing (inner peace), it is usually due to the fact that the memory being dealt with contains anger. Most people have forgiven the best they can and have dealt with the anger cognitively, but they have never forgiven from the heart. How then, do we *"forgive from the heart"* as mentioned in Matthew 18:35? *By forgiving the offense while in the memory where the offense occurred.*

During thousands of hours of helping people find inner peace, we have found the following four steps very effective in the process of forgiveness from the heart. One thing you must understand is that inner healing (peace) will never occur when the memory contains anger, bitterness, hatred, jealously, defiance, belligerence, or any other revengeful feeling.

As Christians, we have the responsibility to get ourselves to the point where we can forgive. Without forgiveness we cannot move forward or get beyond the wall of unforgiveness. God can, and will, give us the unction to forgive from the heart by the power of the Holy Spirit. All things are possible through Christ who strengthens us. However, we need to ask Him for His strengthening. If you don't ask, you will not receive. Study the next four steps and see if it doesn't help you forgive the tough situations in your life.

Forgiveness from the Heart

Step 1. Allow Jesus to show you the root memory or origin of your anger.

The root memory is where the offence occurred. God is the only one that knows for sure where and what it is. There may be several memories you will work on, but it always works best to ask God to show you where the original offence occurred. In the case of multiple memories, work them in the order He shows them to you.

Step 2. Ask Jesus for His power and ability to forgive the offender.

You cannot do it alone if you remain focused on the root memory and the feelings in that memory. Jesus Himself could not forgive the sins which crucified Him without the power of His Father, and neither can we. Therefore, do not let pride take hold of you here, causing you to think you can do it by yourself. It cannot be done alone! Ask Jesus to help you.

Another ploy of the enemy is to make you feel you have already dealt with this, and this is a waste of time. However, if you feel any revengeful feelings in the memory you are dealing with, you have only dealt with it cognitively as mentioned before. As you stay focused on the memory, say, ***"Jesus, I know I need to forgive _______________, but right now I cannot do it alone. Would you please give me your power and ability?"***

After you have asked for His help, keep focusing on the memory and its feeling. You will know you have the Lord's help when you suddenly feel like it is "do-able". It's like you feel the presence of the Lord coming alongside of you in the memory. Suddenly, you just know you can do it.

Step 3. Forgive (release) the offender using the following pattern:

"Jesus, thank you for your help. I choose to forgive _________ because I believe ____________ didn't have a clue how deeply he/she/they hurt me. Therefore, I release __________ to you and ask you to please take this anger and bitterness from me and heal me."

Caution must be exercised here because the enemy does not want you to forgive anyone, nor does your mind. At this point, you may feel very strongly about the fact that the offender did, in fact, know exactly what he/she was doing, and they did know exactly how deeply it hurt you. At the risk of seeming to come to the rescue of the one who hurt you, please allow me to help you understand some things.

First of all, none of us fully understand just how those things we say or do affects eternity. If we did, we wouldn't do or say them. Secondly, your offender may not truly know he/she was hurting you. Thirdly, assuming for a moment that they did know just what they were doing, we must follow the pattern of Jesus if we truly are going to forgive from the heart. Remember, I told you it was impossible to do this alone and, after all, we are talking about becoming *genuine*.

Look for a moment at 1Peter 2:19-23. This section of scripture is dealing with suffering from being mistreated, being accused of those things we really did not do, and being punished for things we were not responsible for. In other words, one suffering at the hands of an offender. Let's look specifically at verse 21.

> *"For to this you were called, because Christ also suffered for us, leaving us an example, that you should follow His steps."* (1Peter 2:21, emphasis added to make a point)

Another scripture for your consideration is found in 1John 2:6:

> *"He who says he abides in Him ought himself also to walk just as He walked."* (1John 2:6)

The point I am trying to make is that we are commanded to follow Jesus' footsteps, which means His example. His way is the only way that works. The enemy and your mind will do everything possible to talk you out of it, but please do not let that happen. I implore you, my friend, to allow the Holy Spirit to help you through and follow these tested and proven steps. You will be glad you did, or you will be terribly sorry you didn't. Do not allow your mind to talk you out of it because it seems too hard or not fair. We are not talking about fairness; we are talking about finding perfect inner peace and spiritual maturity.

I have witnessed many people who followed through and instantly received such release that it was clearly visible on their faces and in their countenance. In just a few seconds, you should physically feel the burden being lifted off of you. In practically every case, the release is accompanied with a long sigh of relief from the one offering the forgiveness because of the weight or pressure being lifted. I am so convinced that you will feel it being lifted that, should you not feel anything, you probably are still holding onto something. In other words, you have not forgiven from the heart. Please try it again, and stay focused on the memory that the Lord showed you. Please! Do not give up!!

Step 4. Thank Jesus for the release. Ask to see any other memories that could cause your anger.

If the Lord shows you another memory, return to Step 2 and work the new memory through as you did this one.

Congratulations! You are on your way to perfect inner peace and becoming genuine. I know that was a very big step and I also know by experience that it will pay big dividends as you continue to *externalize* your anger and *forgive* those who hurt or anger you in the future.

It is time to quit allowing the flesh to have its way. By giving the Lord all your anger, cares, concerns, and general bad feelings, He can then show you where they came from bringing you into His peace. This is the process of becoming a *genuine* Christian.

A Genuine Christian Fits into the House of God

"Coming to Him as to a living stone, rejected indeed by men, but chosen by God and precious, you also, as living stones, are being built up a spiritual house, a holy priesthood, to offer up spiritual sacrifices acceptable to God through Jesus Christ." (1Peter 2:4-5)

Jesus is the Chief Corner Stone, rejected by men but chosen by God to be the Corner Stone and foundation on which all of God's house would stand (1Corinthians 3:11). We as followers of Christ are *living stones,* which the Master builder (Holy Spirit) is fitting together upon the foundation of Jesus Christ. We are a part of the spiritual house as well as the ones offering spiritual sacrifices and proclaiming His praises to the world (1Peter 2:9). You are *genuine,* active living stones in His spiritual structure, as you connect to a physical house (a church) and to its pastor in your local area. Being connected and committed to your church and pastor is the Master Builders physical act of fitting and mortaring the living stones together. Christ the chief

Corner Stone will either become for us a resting place or a stumbling stone — a rock of offense (1Peter 2:8).

Pastors, evangelists, and prophets are to submit to an apostle who is covering and pulling others like them together under a common vision. Apostles must be submitted to and serving an Apostolic Council where your work is overseen and strengthened by your peers and elders. This is the order of God. We cannot expect to receive God's blessings unless we are willing to fit into His Divine order.

This idea that we can submit to Jesus without being a part of a local church is foolish. Refusing to connect to a local church is refusing the very ministry of the Master Builder, the Holy Spirit. Submitting to God's Divine Governmental structure and His plan is being a part of a local church. You cannot be a part of God's plan and not be active in a local church. After all, Jesus died for the church. Isaiah prophesied that *the government of God would always be on His shoulders and the increase of His government and peace there would be no end* (Isaiah 9:6-7).

The local church is called the pillar and foundation of truth in 1Timothy 3:15. Our connection to God (The Holy Spirit) directs and oversees our individual connections to the pillar and foundation of Truth – after all, Jesus is Truth (John 14:6). Not submitting to a local church or believing you need to be sounds like a personal issue or a lack of knowledge to me! Hopefully this book is helping you clear up both possibilities.

The reason many have trouble submitting to a local church is the result of an emotional wound. I have personally ministered to those who, because of taking an offense or feeling they were attacked by someone trusted within the church, ran away from the church rather than stay and work to resolve their issues. Staying and confronting seemed too painful to consider as an option for them. Of course, the devil likes that, so he is going to do all he can to encourage you to run. The problem with the church is that it contains humans just like you and me. We all can and do make mistakes and sometimes those mistakes hurt others, even when the plan was not to injure but to bless. Much of the time, those who hurt you were never aware they hurt you. Running never resolves anything and it begins a life of running.

The devil loves to keep the children of God running from church to church, telling them to find that perfect place where they feel the most comfortable. Comfort is not what you should be looking for. Jesus knows where He wants you, so ask and follow Him. If you are always comfortable, you could be living in apathy. When something confronts you and makes you uncomfortable, be willing to face it and work through the situation with God's help. The willingness to confront your issues helps to guarantee that apathy will not trap you. Use the pressures caused by your local church relationships to drive you to God with the goal of finding His perfect peace. Once you have His peace, then God can equip you to restore others. He is a God of restoration and He has promised to give you a word that will restore (2Corinthians 5:18-19).

Look with me for a minute at this section of scripture. I hear people quote 2Corinthians 5:17 all the time. I wonder if they know just what the Holy Spirit is teaching here and what qualifies them to claim this scripture for themselves. If you are running from church to church or are unwilling to confront those who have hurt you and to work through the interpersonal relationships that come your way, you are not personally living out this scripture. It is good to quote scripture but it is better to live it out. Now, before you pick up stones to hurl my way, stick with me for just a minute and I will help you.

"Therefore, if anyone is in Christ he is a new creation; old

> *things have passed away; behold, all things have become new."* (2Corinthians 5:17)

This scripture is talking about you, the person who needs to confront their issues and possibly the one stirring you up. Let's start at the front of this teaching.

> *"For the love of Christ compels us..."*
> (2Corinthians 5:14)

Everything we do must spring out of our love for what Jesus did and is doing for us. He loves us right where we are in life. That love He has for us should be the motivation for everything we do. That is what motivates *genuine* Christians; therefore, because He died for all of mankind, He also died for the ones we need to confront, or the ones triggering our pain. If we are accepting His death for our benefit, then we can no longer live for ourselves, but rather for Him who died for us. In other words, our actions now reflect directly on Jesus Christ.

> *"Therefore, from now on, we regard no one according to the flesh. Even though we have known Christ according to the flesh, yet now we know Him thus no longer."* (2Corinthians 5:16)

Because of the Spirit of Christ in us, we no longer need nor are we free to make decisions or judgments about another person based upon their actions toward us. No matter what another person makes us feel, we cannot use that fleshly feeling to direct or justify our actions. Feelings will *help you* find out *what is in you* if you don't run from them or hide them. We cannot run just because someone hurt our feelings or made us angry. We cannot disappear just because of something the pastor said that made us feel something negative. We are of Christ Jesus, His spirit lives in us, and *Jesus died for all* — not just for you and me. As we enjoy that favored position with the Lord, we must also realize that it carries a responsibility with it. That responsibility is to live *in Him* who made it all possible.

> *"Therefore, if anyone is in Christ, he is a new creation; old things have passed away; behold, all things have become new."* (2Corinthians 5:17)

When we take offense, we are making a judgment about the other person. An offense is your unwillingness to tell the offender about your feelings. You instead, internalize your anger or your feelings, which causes you to become offended and bitter. It also causes another problem; it keeps you from setting your own boundaries, which does not help the offender or keep him from offending you again. In other words, if you refuse to tell him he offended you he may never know. If you do not confront the person, how do you expect him to know he crossed one of your boundaries? Confronting him/her is helping him grow in his own life.

A healthy response to all local church struggles is to confront the issue, and explain how it made you feel. When you speak up, another important thing happens to you, all the pressure of the offense leaves you. However, don't stop there. Tell the Lord what you feel and allow Him to work you through the issue first. Confronting is not attacking; it is educating and healing. If you feel you must attack, fear is driving you. Tell the Lord you are afraid and allow perfect Love (Jesus) to drive the fear away (1John 4:18) first and then confront the one who offended you.

Look at it this way: your greatest allies are those in your life (including those in your church) who cause you the most stress. Why? Because every bad feeling is proof, you believe a lie about yourself and Jesus needs the pressures put on you by others to help you find inner healing and ultimately, His peace and maturity. Rejoice, my friend, and stay in your local church. If you sense God is trying to move you, allow Him to direct you to where He wants you. Don't take it on yourself to go looking. When God directs you to the place he wants you, get grounded and work to fit in to their vision and purpose. If God takes you to another church, it will be to help accomplish that pastor's vision, not to install your own. Become a healing agent for the Lord and bless your church and community.

Once again, 1Peter 2:5 tells us we are *living stones* fitting together into a *spiritual house.* Stones of any house or building must *fit tight* together so the house or building can stand. One of the things that cause stress fractures between the living stones of the church, ultimately causing the stones to separate, is the battle for position. This many times, is from an innocent desire on the part of zealous workers to accomplish something within the Body of Christ. But it can also stem from an unhealthy desire for power or position. Regardless of the cause, it is important to understand the scriptures concerning this subject.

"A man's gift makes room for him, and brings him before great men" (Proverbs 18:16). "For exaltation (promotion) comes neither from the east nor from the west nor from the south. But God is the Judge: He puts down one, and exalts another" (Psalm 75:6, 7, comments added).

You may feel you can do better than the pastor, worship-leader, teacher, or elders but it was the person's gift and God that put him or her there. Remember, because our life is an ongoing project, we must always submit to the plans and desires of God.

There may, in fact, be a call on your life to pastor, lead worship, teach, or lead some committee but allow God to speak to your leadership and point you out. If you feel that no one will notice you unless you say something, ask God to reveal the origin of that feeling. Once He identifies the origin for you, work through the lies He uncovers and find His peace. Remember, you brought that feeling with you. The church did not create it. Submit to your church's vision as though it was your own and you will become qualified for promotion. Actually, if you cannot work to fulfill another man's vision and serve that man and body in the doing of it, you will never qualify to receive your own. Those adequately trained to lead are those who serve well.

When a pastor takes it upon himself to promote because of the person's special talent or the fear that he may lose the person to another church, he puts himself in a very dangerous position — between God and the person in question. Submit the fear of not promoting that person to God. Allow Him to show you why you feel inadequate or intimidated. That pressure is to help you, the leader, to lead as *God* gives you the direction. The person who feels they need promoted is dealing with inner emotions that only God can help them overcome. Promoting them prematurely is a future disaster for them and the church. When it is promotion time for that person, God will tell the pastor or leader first.

When I recognized the call on my life, I was serving a pastor of a small country church by doing everything I could do to make that church a comfortable place that others would want to attend. I knew in my heart that God had more for me to do than mow the yard, clean up the building, and pick up after others. However, to my benefit, I didn't think I qualified for more. One day the pastor asked me to meet him at the church to set up some chairs for a special meeting. I knew in my heart that the pastor was going to ask me to work as his assistant. As I was setting up the chairs and cleaning the room the pastor said, "Come over her and sit down. I have something I must tell you." During that meeting, he told me that God had instructed him to train me for the next four years and then install me as the pastor of that church. I knew what he was going to say even though I didn't qualify at that time. God had personally prepared me to receive that word as well as led the pastor to deliver it to me. I was not looking for a promotion and the pastor was not looking for an assistant.

Pastors, please do not put yourself and your church in jeopardy by promoting someone into a position that God has not first pointed out. If there is a question concerning someone's call, ask God to verify it. He will verify it or help you understand what is going on. He will also tell you how to help that person prepare and through you, He will develop the workers and leaders you need.

The feelings produced from not receiving a promotion or being noticed are there for a reason. The emotional pain you experience is indicating you are not yet qualified to lead because there is obviously something within you that God desires to help you overcome. Maybe it is pride or selfishness. Maybe it is something hidden so deep you would never guess or find it on your own. Only the Lord knows what it is and how it would ultimately become your downfall.

When a person fails because they would not pay attention to God's warnings, it not only destroys your ministry but your witness for Christ, the trust others built in you and possibly your life. Please keep in mind that we are on a journey to becoming *genuine* followers of Christ. If that is where you are, then you need to follow Him by communicating with Him. When you feel unnoticed, the fear of falling behind or the anger these feelings generate, tell God. Cast those cares upon him (2 Peter 5:7). Allow Him to show you where they began and how to rid yourself of them. Believe me when I say, you definitely want to get victory over those feelings *before* you take leadership. It's much safer now than when you become responsible for others and their actions. Remember the warning that says, *"My brethren, let not many of you become teachers, knowing that we shall receive a stricter judgment"* (James 3:1). Don't rush it. Let God lead, prepare, heal and open the doors for you.

God's plan is that the local church becomes a positive influence in their community, thereby attracting others from the community. The locals within the individual communities need their churches in order to gather and learn from one another. There is safety and encouragement in numbers. The Apostle Paul commented on the importance of the local church this way. *"And let us consider one another in order to stir up love and good works, not forsaking the assembling of ourselves together, as in the manner of some, but exhorting one another, and so much the more as you see the Day approaching"* (Hebrews 10:24, 25).

As we gather in our local churches, we naturally encourage each other and together we are stronger and can accomplish much more than, if we abide alone. When you feel down and discouraged there will always be someone in your local church who will help you become encouraged. When you need help God will make sure there will be someone there who can help you. Affirmation is the most important emotional need every human has. Much of that need can be satisfied as you *faithfully* serve in your local church. However, some people will fail to tell you they appreciate you. When that happens you can find the affirmation you need by simply telling God how you feel. He will help you feel appreciated. He will meet needs within you that others will not or cannot.

As a pastor, I can tell you first hand that, you have the power to warm the heart of your pastor, helping him recognize his life really counts for something, as you remain faithful to your local church. Serving as pastor is not an easy job. Good pastors work hard to hear and follow God for their flock. They pray and watch over your spiritual good even when they are under personal attack. They are there to lift you even when they feel they are in the bottom of the pit. They are there to teach and encourage you even when life hands them much discouragement. You have equal power to discourage him and in extreme cases, which I have witnessed, ultimately destroy him. If you are not faithful, you are a discouragement to him. If you are always finding fault with him and the work he is doing, God is not looking too kindly upon you right now. If you are struggling with fitting and settling into your local church, I would be talking to God if I were you and getting the reason exposed and healed.

As your pastor goes about doing the work God called him to do, you will never notice his difficulties. He will be there faithfully for you when you need him. However, he is not a machine. He needs your love and encouragement as much as you need his.

Pastors, if you have a habit of complaining or more than occasionally mentioning the needs and troubles you are having, please consider this question. Are you concerned or afraid that your need will go unmet? I have heard more than one pastor quote with great volume and intensity that *my God shall meet all my need in accordance with His riches in Glory by Christ Jesus* (Philippians 4:19) while in the same breath complain or drop hints that they are in need or are suffering in one way or another. That action is not an act of faith to which God can respond. Nothing aggravates me more and does more damage to the Kingdom of God than a preacher who spends half of his sermon time preaching faith and the other half dropping hints and promising special blessings to those who will respond to his needs. If you really believe that God will meet all your needs in accordance with His riches in glory by Christ Jesus, you will find it impossible to drop hints or complain. If you are that unsure of God's love for you, you need to be talking to Him about what you truly feel. We preachers have the power to encourage the Body of Christ to be faithful to the church. Let's not discourage them by our own doubts and fears.

Genuine Christians are encouraging by being faithful, committed and connected to one another through their local church.

The Genuine Christian Understands We Were Chosen to Praise God

> *"But you are a chosen generation, a royal priesthood, a holy nation, and His own special people, that you may proclaim the praises of Him ..."* (1Peter 1:9)

Genuine Christians love to praise God. The Scriptures teach us to praise Him (Psalm 67). Powerful things happen when God's children gather and praise Him. The Bible teaches us that God inhabits the praises of His people (Psalm 22:3). Psalm 111 and 112 teach us that God has special provision for those who praise and worship Him. The *genuine* ones love the praise and worship portion of the church service. However, I have seen people purposefully miss the first part of a church service because they do not want to stand and praise God. Can you imagine that?

If you are one of those who dislike or feel uncomfortable during the praise and worship time, you need to get help identifying the cause of it. You are missing some of the greatest joy in your life. I guarantee your dislike of worship and praise is being driven by a feeling that is rooted somewhere in your mind. By submitting that feeling to the Lord, you are allowing Him to show you where it started and free you from the thief that is stealing your ability to receive His joy. The joy of the Lord is our strength and worshipping and praising Him gives God great joy, as well as those offering Him praise.

Others may not enjoy the praise and worship portion of a service because many are looking to man (pastor or praise and worship team) to bring them into the presence of God. They think that if they do not feel God's presence it must be the fault of the worship team or the pastor. They expect man to do for them what they must do themselves. It takes disciplining our bodies before our spirits can communicate with God. It must be something we, as spirit people, make our bodies do.

Sometimes people have a tough time worshiping because they are too busy looking around at what everyone else is doing. Put your mind on Him and you won't be drawn away; again, discipline your flesh.

There are others afraid of what everyone else might think of them when they attempt to express themselves to God. If you are afraid of what people might be thinking of you, you need to tell God what you are feeling and allow Him to speak to that issue. During the worship service would be a good time to communicate to God about the feelings that are keeping you away from worshipping Him.

You may be thinking, "You mean I don't have to sing along with the song leader to properly worship God?" You don't have to sing at all to worship. Worship is communicating your love and adoration for God to God. If you are unable to do that, let God help you understand why. If the words of the song express what my heart needs to say to God, I will sing the song. However, if my heart needs to hear from the Lord on another issue or if I have the desire to express a different message than the song is expressing, I talk to Him in an attitude of worship. Once I have expressed myself to Him or asked the question I need Him to address, I then listen for His reply. Once I sense His reply, I then speak back to Him what I received from Him.[9] During worship and praise time, both you and God should receive something from each other and it is up to you to see that both are refreshed. Once you are refreshed and you sense God's presence, you are spiritually and emotionally ready to receive the preached Word. When everything is in the proper order, you will not be able to miss receiving what you need.

If you just sing the songs and mouth the words others are mouthing, you may not even be worshiping God. You are just doing a religious exercise. Worship is the time for us to be expressive to God about how we feel toward Him. Don't get trapped into a religious routine that does nothing for you. If it does nothing for you, it does nothing for God either.

Take the worship time to be expressive to God, keeping your eyes on Him only, and honor Him with your expressions

---

[9] For a complete understanding of why we must speak audibly to God when He speaks to us, refer to Appendix I, *Why Must We Speak Audibly To God?"*

of love, adoration or even questions – regardless of the direction the worship leader is leading. The only thing you don't want to do is to draw attention to yourself. Worshiping God makes it all about God and not the worshipers. Make sure you are worshiping Him and not your ability to express yourself. Have fun during the praise and worship time — relax and enjoy the time and you will soon be enjoying His presence. When your physical body begins to feel the presence of the Lord, all the struggle of getting there quickly melts away.

If you never physically feel the presence of the Lord, while you are worshiping Him, make sure that your mind stays fixed on Him only. Regardless of whether you sing or speak to Him, raise your hands, sit down, dance, or just meditate on Him in silence; make sure that you keep Him as the center of your motivation. Too many people allow every thought that comes along to enter their mind and destroy what God needs to do for them. Make sure you make your mind behave and concentrate on Him. Fix Him in your mind's eye and do not let that image or thought escape you. Worship Him and you will soon physically feel His presence with you. When that becomes normal in your church, the Lord's corporate anointing will begin to accomplish things that make all the efforts worthwhile. When the corporate anointing is strong, it becomes impossible to contain your "Praise the Lords" and your "Hallelujahs."

Those who say, "Praise the Lord!" all day long are not necessarily *genuine;* however, those who are *genuine* do find many occasions throughout every day to say praise the Lord. When you are genuinely in love with God, you will see many of His blessings in some of the strangest experiences.

The Bible teaches that, "Every good gift and every perfect gift is from above, and comes down from the Father of lights, with whom there is no variation or shadow of turning" (James

1:17). I mention this to possibly help solve some confusion people have when it comes to rejoicing and praising the Lord for the things that happen in our life.

A general rule to follow is, if it is *good* and *perfect* it is from God. I have heard well-meaning Christians praise God for sickness or accidents. When confronted about why they chose to praise God for problems, they said they believe that everything comes from God because of His sovereignty. They reasoned therefore, that God could have stopped it but didn't, so He must be trying to teach them something with circumstance.

If that testimony draws people to God, I'll eat my hat. That is not what the Bible teaches. Someone confused in their doctrine, because they do not understand God's character, taught that idea. If what they say is true, then the scripture I just quoted in James is a lie. Luke 10:19 would also be a lie; *"For I have given you authority to trample on snakes and scorpion and nothing by any means shall harm you."*

Now, I am not saying that bad things should never happen to God's children. Bad things do come into our lives occasionally, but God does not send them. For instance, Jesus went to the cross to pay the price for our physical and emotional health, (1Peter 2:24, Matthew 8:16, 17). If God, our Father, puts sickness on us to teach us something: then Jesus died in vain, we are sinning when we go to the doctor, and Jesus was sinning when he healed all those He healed while on the earth (Matthew 8:16b, 17).

Jesus' work on the cross also made a way for us to enjoy prosperity (3John 2). Therefore, if God puts poverty on us, Jesus' payment must not have been enough. That is foolish! Jesus' work on the cross was more than sufficient for any of our problems and challenges in life.

With His Name comes all the authority of Heaven. He expects us to use this authority rather than, taking life as it comes and then, blaming Him for not doing enough to protect us. Someone not paying attention usually causes accidents, therefore, we must quit blaming God by thinking He is the source of our misfortunes.

The Bible tells us: *"See then that you walk circumspectly, not as fools but as wise..."* (Ephesians 5:15). Being circumspectly paints the picture of one who has eyes all around their head; nothing gets by them because they are alert. "How can God expect us to be that alert?" you ask. Because the Holy Spirit never slumbers or sleeps and is always aware of everything coming into and out of our lives.

We need to pay more close attention, recognizing God is for us and will always warn us and instruct us. We must become more in tune with the Holy Spirit within us. Our responsibility is to obey what He instructs. One who follows the Holy Spirit is a *genuine* Christian — anything less than that, the Bible calls *unwise* (Ephesians 5:15-17).

The Bible also teaches that what we do not know can kill us (Hosea 4:6). Ignorance is not bliss, it is dangerous. Unless sickness and disease is a *good* and *perfect gift,* it cannot come from God. Sickness and disease comes from our enemy, just like ignorance, poverty, and human disasters.

God is not yet in the judging business (John 3:17), so He cannot be sending natural disasters to teach sinners a lesson. That is ridiculous. Come on, Friend. We must walk with Him, talk with Him, and get to know Him before we allow someone to convince us He is in the business of destruction and human torture. God is in the business of LIFE so PRAISE HIM!

A time is coming when the earth will fall to judgment and the earth will know it. God's judgment is not God destroying in order to get even with His enemy. What we have understood as *God's judgment* is actually man reaping the unrighteousness he himself has planted (Romans 1:28-32, 2:5).

From the very beginning, much of mankind has rejected God's interaction with him on the earth. The ultimate proof that mankind wants no connection to a living God was the decision and action of crucifying His only begotten Son, Jesus Christ. Man's rejection continues as he continues pushing God and everything that reminds him of God out of his life. We are not supposed to pray and mention the name of Jesus in schools and other public gatherings. We no longer can see nativity scenes in or around our government properties. The Ten Commandments no longer grace courtroom walls and public statues.

Man keeps pushing Jesus (God) out and one day God will pull everyone waiting for Him off this earth. When that happens, man finally gets what he wants, he thinks. However, no man is ready for the hell that will befall this earth when God's presence is gone. When there is no God to protect this earth from the hordes of hell, mankind reaps what he has sown and the judgments, or results (Revelations 4-20), will make the natural disasters we have been witnessing look like Sunday school picnics. However, when that happens I will not be here and neither will any *genuine* Christian. So praise Him and praise Him and praise Him some more! The most important thing we can do right now is to get serious with God and become *genuine*. We have a lot of work to do and a lot of fun will be had doing it so let's be about making sure we are up to the challenge.

Genuine Christians are Submissive to Authorities

> *"Therefore submit yourselves to every ordinance of man for the Lord's sake, whether to the king as supreme, or to governors ..."* (1Peter 2:13-14)

Romans 13:1 teaches "Let every soul be subject to the governing authorities. For there is no authority except from God, and the authorities that exist are appointed by God."

God does not hold kindly to those who will not obey the laws established by our governing officials. You may not like the laws, but if you are counting on becoming *genuine* as a Christian, you must submit to them and obey them for the following two, very good reasons:

> *"Therefore whoever resists the authority resists the ordinance of God, and those who resist will bring judgment on themselves. For he is God's minister to you for good ..... But if you do evil, be afraid; for he does not bear the sword in vain; for he is God's minister, an avenger to execute*

> *wrath on him who practices evil."* (Romans 13:2, 4, emphasis added)

> *"For this is the will of God, that by doing good you may put to silence the ignorance of foolish men—as free, yet not using liberty as a cloak for vice, but as bondservants of God. Honor all people. Love the brotherhood. Fear God. Honor the king."* (1Peter 2:15-17, emphasis added)

We are ambassadors for Christ, as though God were pleading through us (2Corinthians 5:20a). He, in fact, is pleading to a lost and broken world through us, His servants. It is our responsibility to show the world that our God is alive and worth knowing. Obeying Him and being submissive and respectful to the authorities is a vital part of our witness as *genuine* Christians (Acts 1:8). Living our witness for Him speaks much louder than what we say about Him. In fact, we speak volumes against Him when our actions do not line up with our message.

Not obeying will not only bring reproach on the Name of Christ, but will also open the door and allow evil to enter our lives. We wonder why bad things happen to good people and sometimes, not always, it's because those we were regarding as good may not be as good as we think.

> *"Do not be deceived, God is not mocked; for whatever a man sows, that he will also reap. For he who sows to his flesh will of the flesh reap corruption, but he who sows to the Spirit will of the Spirit reap everlasting life."* (Galatians 6:7)

To be submissive means, we are first submissive to the things of God. Using our freedom in Christ for opportunity to sin will open the door to evil that will affect you in a very negative way. It doesn't matter whether others know it or not, it will open the door to trouble. Being submissive to God means, you are respectful and submissive to those God has established as authorities above us. For example: our national, regional, and local authorities, church leaders, officers of the law, mothers and fathers, legal guardians, etc. Anyone whose responsibility it is to look out for your best interest and good.

Through the Apostle Paul, the Holy Spirit speaks very clearly how a *genuine* Christian should respect and respond to our political leaders.

> *"Therefore I exhort first of all that supplications, prayers, intercessions, and giving of thanks be made for all men, for kings (presidents) and all who are in authority (federal, state, and local leaders), that we may lead a quiet and peaceable life in all godliness and reverence. For this is good and acceptable in the sight of God our Savior, who desires all men to be saved and to come to the knowledge of the truth."* (1Timothy 2:1-4, comments added)

Look for a minute at the three points made in this section of scripture. First, we are to pray for and give thanks for all of our leaders. It doesn't say just those whom you happen to agree with. I get so tired of hearing people bash our leaders. If you don't agree with them, we are fortunate to have godly ways to deal with them. Thank God, we live in a country where we can voice our opinions and offer suggestions and vote. Good honest dialogue is healthy and constructive. However, to bash our leaders and to smear their character and their name just because you disagree with them or their ideologies totally goes against everything the Bible teaches. You might say it is anti-Christ. After all, we have already seen in Romans 13:1 that

God appoints all leaders. When bad, ungodly leadership takes control it is a sure sign Christians have not been doing enough praying or tending to their responsibilities. That leads me to the second point made in 1Timothy 2:1-4.

Paul said that if we pray and give thanks for all our leadership we will lead a quiet and peaceable life. When we are leading a quiet and peaceable life it is a sure sign godly leaders are in control.

> *"Righteousness exalts a nation, but sin is a reproach to any people."* (Proverbs 14:34)

> *"By the blessing of the upright the city (or nation) is exalted, but it is overthrown by the mouth of the wicked."* (Proverbs 11:11)

> *"When the righteous rejoice, there is great glory; but when the wicked arise, men hide themselves."* (Proverbs 28:12)

If we Christians tend to our responsibilities, we can expect to see godly leadership with a righteous agenda lead our cities, states, and our nation. If we join in with those who bash leadership, we are going to endure the wrath of God because ungodly leadership will take over.

The third point made in 1Timothy 2 is found in verses three and four.

> *"For this is good and acceptable in the sight of God our Savior, <u>who desires all men to be saved and to come to the knowledge of the truth</u>."* (1Timothy 2:3, 4 emphases added)

As we tend to our responsibilities of praying for, encouraging and being thankful for our leaders not only will God smile on our cities, states, and our nation, but also the knowledge of the truth will spread and people will be saved because of it. Can you imagine the headache we will give the enemies of God when we begin to take our responsibilities as *genuine* Christians seriously?

> *"If My people who are called by My name will humble themselves, and pray and seek My face, and turn from their wicked ways, then I will hear from heaven, and will forgive their sin and heal their land."* (2Chronicles 7:14)

It takes humility to pray for and give thanks for some leaders who just do not represent our values; however, that is the way to turn them over to God. It is His responsibility to heal our land. It is our responsibilities to humble ourselves, pray, quit complaining about and bashing our leaders and repent so He can heal and restore righteousness to our land. G*enuine* Christians will rule our nation as we give thanks for and pray for our lcadcrs.

Being respectful and obedient to the authorities and the laws many times brings pressure upon us for a reason. I have known people who, for instance, hated it when they had to stop at a red light. Riding with them was amazing in a very negative way. Every stoplight offered them a challenge that told them they were either a winner or a loser. If someone got in front of them and caused them to miss the light they would make a scene about the "*stupid driver* and how they ought to learn to drive before they are issued a license." I have watched as people habitually broke every speed limit. They could not drive within the limit of the law. I am talking about Christians.

Some even had the Christian fish symbol on the back of their car or a bumper sticker drawing people to their church or reminding them of their need of Jesus.

This kind of behavior stems from emotional wounds triggered by, in this case, traffic laws and/or other drivers. A red light, a speed limit, or generally being controlled by others triggers something in their memory that brings alive within them a negative feeling which, in turn, drives them to act unreasonably negative. This is where road rage comes from, physical and verbal altercations, acts of physical abuse, and murders of passion.

The root of the problem is the triggered feeling. As Christians, we need to deal with our negative feelings by telling the Lord what it is we are feeling. Too many times we merely excuse ourselves by thinking or saying, "Oh well, that's just who I am so you are going to have to deal with it!" In other words, I'm not going to change and if you can't handle my misbehavior, it's your problem not mine. That kind of response, my friend, is childishness and will get you into deep trouble unless you recognize the danger that living in denial will cause you and the others around you.

I've heard people say, "God loves me just the way I am." This is their way to justify misbehavior. Well, God does love you the way you are, but He is not too keen about leaving any of us the way we are. His desire is to change all of us to be more responsive and responsible in life. However, He cannot help us change unless we are willing to look at ourselves honestly and then get honest with Him. If a little pressure (a red stop light) doesn't cause us to seek His help you can expect the pressure to increase (a traffic ticket) until we finally realize we need His help. Hopefully this happens before something serious or tragic occurs.

Genuine Christians pay attention to the messages their feelings (emotions) send them. God is trying to get your attention to spare you from more than you can handle on your own. It's time we wise up and begin to get real with life. It's time we wake up and recognize that feelings are telling us something and God is trying desperately to help us.

The choice of when we turn to Him is ours, so my suggestion is, as you recognize the symptoms, turn to Him immediately. Isaiah's instruction says it this way, *"Seek the Lord while He may be found, call upon Him while He is near."* (Isaiah 55:6) In other words, allow your daily pressures to become stepping-stones rather than allowing them to grow into mountains that may eventually crush you.

The Genuine Christians Live a Higher Standard

> *"For to this you were called, because Christ also suffered for us, leaving us an example, that you should follow His steps."* (1Peter 2:21)

We have some big shoes to fill; much bigger than we can fill in our own power. To generally follow Jesus from a religious perspective is one thing, but as one desiring to become a *genuine* Christian in everyday life, it becomes an entirely different challenge. Look at the details Peter spelled out that we are to follow.

> *"Who committed no sin, nor was deceit found in His mouth; who, when He was reviled, did not revile in return; when He suffered He did not threaten, but committed Himself to Him who judges righteously."* (1Peter 2:22, 23, emphasis added)

According to Hebrews 4, Jesus never committed any sin. "... *but was in all points tempted as we are, yet without sin*" (Hebrews 4:15b) He was tempted in every way we are yet, He never submitted to the pressure to sin. He never lied or was deceitful to anyone.

Life continually hands all of us the opportunity to stretch or conceal the truth. When that opportunity comes knocking, there is always a little voice telling us that it would be better if we were to lie just a little bit in order to save someone's feelings or to save our own hide. The world's philosophy is that a little lie occasionally can be healthy. Jesus had the same temptations, but never gave in to them. People were always cursing Jesus out, mouthing off to Him, correcting or reviling Him when there were no reasons to correct Him. Can you imagine cursing out Jesus to His face? Unfortunately, I am sure the Name "Jesus" was a curse word even when He was on the earth. After all, history tells us that being called a Christian, in the first century after Jesus' death, was considered an insult by those in the world and many times led to the recipients death.

Jesus never responded to get even with their railings once. "...*When He was reviled, did not revile in return...*" He was quiet and peaceful, which probably aggravated His attackers more than if He had reviled them in return, but thank God He didn't. One more point, He never threatened them with anything. Can you imagine how wonderful a world this would be if people wouldn't lie to one another, revile and threaten one another? Well, that's the way the Kingdom of God should be. And eventually it will be.

> "*To this <u>you</u> were called...<u>you</u> should follow His steps.*"
> (1Peter 2:21, emphasis added)

How in the world did Jesus go through all He went through without trying to get even or threatening anyone even once? He did it the same way you and I are to get through this life. *By committing Himself to Him who judges righteously* (1Peter 2:23b).

He trusted His heavenly Father, the only one who judges righteously, the only one who can be trusted. He knew his emotions could not be trusted as He lived through all the challenges that life was handing Him. He knew He could not control His emotions any more than you or I can. He knew He could not control what His emotions would cause him to do. The enemy was counting on Jesus' emotions getting the best of Him, blowing the whole plan. If Jesus had slipped even once, He would not have qualified as our Messiah. He had to be a perfect, spotless Lamb without blemish.

The power of a lie is such that Jesus could not afford to believe even one lie about His person or His purpose. One lie is all it would take to create the *emotional issue* or *button* that, when pushed by His enemies, would have caused Him to respond from His emotional pain (reflex) rather than purposefully following His Fathers instructions. One lie would have caused His feelings to overwhelm His passion, destroying His purpose, leaving the world without a Redeemer. I am convinced that is what He meant when He told His disciples,

> *"...The ruler of this world is coming, and he has nothing <u>in</u> me."* (John 14:30b, emphasis added)

In other words, Jesus was saying: none of the enemy's plans, the religious system, and the direct attacks from the devil himself caused me to believe a lie. Staying connected to His Father, by the Holy Spirit, allowed Him to continuously receive truth for each of His experiences. Not believing the world's lies is overcoming the world (John 16:33). Jesus gave us the pattern we are to follow and then He set the goal before us (John 13:34).

> *"When He was reviled, did not revile in return; when He suffered, He did not threaten, but committed Himself to Him who judges righteously."* (1Peter 2:23, emphasis added)

When Christians slip and allow their emotions to drive them in the wrong direction, many have the attitude of, "Oh well, what do you expect, after all, we are only human." Many also say in times like this, "Thank God for His grace." The problem with this is the non-believers see our misbehaviors and our casual attitude, which gives them the excuse they need, to stay out of the Body of Christ. "After all, they are no better than I am," they reason, and "Why do I need the church, they act just like me. They are no better than I am." How many people, may actually refuse to meet the Savior because of some lame excuse used for our poor behavior and bad choices?

We are not merely human! We are humans who have been incarnated by the Living God — the Creator of heaven and earth. There is a call on all Christians to walk this higher walk (1John 2:6) and we are empowered to do so successfully (Acts 1:8). The common comment of, "Oh well, what do you expect. After all, I'm only human!" is made as a justification for bad behavior — a coping mechanism. It is a carnal or uninformed person's method of getting the pressure of the moment off of him or redirected to someone else.

> *"Because I live, you will live also. At that day you will know that I am in My Father and you in me and I in*

you." (John 14:19b, 20, emphasis added)

The *day* Jesus was speaking of is the day we begin to *believe* the works Jesus did is exactly the works He expects us to do, with the potential of even greater works (John 14:12). It is the day we truly *believe* that whatever we ask the Father in Jesus' Name He will do (John 14:13, 14). It is the day we *believe* and truly appreciate that Jesus did send us a Helper and He has not left us alone (John 14:16). It is the day that we begin to *believe* and *obey* or follow his immediate commands (*entolē*)[10] spoken to us by our Helper (John 14:21). It is the day we begin to *walk in Jesus' perfect peace* with no inner turmoil or fear (John 14:27). It is the day we truly overcome the world (John 16:33). *That is the day we begin to believe we are more than just mere humans.*

We are the children of the Divine, the King's kids, the elect of all human beings! We are much more than mere mortal human flesh and it is time we begin to live like it. The world needs us to get our act together and represent our Father in Heaven as He deserves.

---

[10] The Greek word translated as commands or commandments in this case is entolē, number 1785 in Strong's. The definition of this word is; "a command, whether of God or man, an authoritative prescription or precept, an immediate command or directive." For further help refer to the chapter entitled; "Understanding the Love Walk."

> *"Lord, who may abide in your tabernacle? Who may dwell in your holy hill? He who walks uprightly, and works righteousness, and speaks truth in his heart; He who does not backbite with his tongue, Nor does evil to his neighbor, nor does he take up a reproach against his friend; he who swears to his own hurt and does not change."* (Psalm 15:1, 2, 3, 4b, emphasis added)

Supernatural power is available to all New Testament Christians (Acts 1:8), to live the instructions found in Psalm 15. When you promise to do something or agree to help someone, please do what you have promised. Even if it ends up costing you, do it anyway. The entire world is watching and measuring us by what we proclaim as truth.

When a *genuine* Christian promises or agrees to do something, he or she always follows through. Nothing is more aggravating than a person who will agree to do something and then fails to complete it at all or in a timely manner. We must be people of our word.

The Bible tells us to let our yes be yes and our no be no (Matthew 5:37). Yes does not mean unless something better or easier comes along. Yes does not mean maybe, if I can get around to it. Yes does not mean when it suites me. And yes does not mean when it is convenient. It means YES. If you need to say, "Yes, when I get around to it, or when it suits me, or when it is convenient." Then you can do it at your convenience. But when you say YES, do it.

Many also have the bad habit of blaming everyone else for their bad feelings and the resulting bad behavior. This also makes the non-believer wonder why he has a need for a relationship with the Savior. Jesus promised us the ability to live in

His peace (John 14:27, 16:33) regardless of what life does to us or does not do for us. If we are unable to live above inner turmoil or fear, then Jesus lied. If we are unwilling *to learn how* to live above inner turmoil or fear, then we really have no good news to proclaim to the world.

The church's basic perspective of salvation needs to change to line up with Gods. From God's perspective, our salvation is more about what God needs to *do for others through us* than for what He can do for us. The church has worked hard, hoping to get God to do things for us as much or more than through us. Unfortunately, in many Christian circles, individuals receive attention based upon what God has done for them, while the things God has done through them goes pretty much unnoticed most of the time.

It's time things change. It's time for the *genuine* Christians to step up to the plate and show the world what serving a living God can really do for our everyday life. Rather than building strongholds that are more elaborate in order to excuse ourselves, we must begin to see that our issues are causing the Kingdom of God and the cause of Christ problems. The reason God has given us faith and the ability to increase our faith is more for helping us deal with our issues than acquiring more stuff. It is time we begin to use our faith for the purpose intended.

We have the same tools available to us that Jesus had when He was physically on this earth. We have a better covenant, based upon a surer guarantee and sealed with the precious blood of Christ. We have the Name that is above every name and the authority that is behind that Name. We have a live-in Comforter and Counselor who has promised to never leave us or forsake us and to tell us everything the Father and Jesus wants us to know. He is here to show us things yet to come, to remind us of everything Jesus has spoken to us, and to be our minute-to-minute connection to Heaven (John 16:13). We have all this going for us and yet, we seem to find it easier to make excuses for our fears and issues; rather than get honest and allow the Holy Spirit to deal with them as they come up. Come on, church, we can and must do better than this.

It's time for us to stand up, and become responsible men and women of God. Responsible people learn how to work with the Lord in order to live in that high level of inner peace that Jesus gives those who turn to Him. After all, the whole world is waiting to see you and I receive what is coming to us, and I believe the moment is now.

> *"For the earnest expectation of the creation eagerly waits for the revealing of the sons of God."* (Romans 8:19)
>
> *"The whole creation is on tiptoe to see the wonderful sight of the sons of God coming into their own."* (Romans 8:19 Phillips Translation)

What is a son of God? A son of God is an average Christian who has had it with the phony promises of religion and is willing to be led by the Spirit of God only (Romans 8:14). One who is finished with hiding behind his or her phony plastic Christian smiley face of "everything's A-OK," and "If I don't admit how I feel no one will ever know and then I will really be OK."

We Christians boast, and rightfully so, that our God is alive. We sing songs to celebrate that our God reigns and He is "alive, alive, alive for ever more". But, I am afraid that the non-Christian world does not see it because the majority of the

Christian community has the same problems, fears, phobias and failures the non-Christians have.

What good does it do to serve a living God if we never take our issues to Him and allow Him to help us overcome? He might as well still be a dead man on a cross or a baby in a manger for all the good He is doing much of the Christian world. I thank God He isn't dead, but what good does it do to tell the world that our God lives and then go right on fumbling around in the dark like the rest of the world does. We serve a LIVING GOD and I believe it is time we begin to show it. That will happen when we begin to get honest with Him and ourselves and begin to live up to the higher standard of our calling. We have the ability through Him, to line up to His standard. We just need to learn how.

For a while, the Christian community wore necklaces, bracelets, bumper stickers, and tee shirts with the letters "WWJD" emboldened upon them. I assumed that meant that those wearing these bold letters were going to do what Jesus would do in the tense, tough trials and temptations of their life. However, it seemed the Christian community had no idea of what Jesus would do because there was no evidence of anything changing in the mass of lives announcing this good intention. When I asked people, "What would Jesus do in this or that particular situation?" I never once received a solid answer from anyone. And believe me I asked many people that question. As an example, we have had well over two thousand private sessions in a period of thirty months, and that doesn't include time spent in front of churches and conferences. However, when asked that question, very few people knew what Jesus would do, and those who seemed like they might know were never confident in their answer. They would stutter and stammer, saying things like, "Well, I'm not sure. It would depend, I suppose, upon..." and never was there a solid answer of confidence that, *this* is what Jesus would do.

Well, let me tell you what Jesus would do in *every* situation. He would speak to His Father and do what His Father told Him to do. If He heard nothing, He would do nothing. How do I know?

> *"My food is to do the will of Him who sent me, and to finish His work."* (John 4:34)

> *"... I do not seek my own will but the will of the Father who sent me."* (John 5:30b)

> *"For I have come down from heaven, not to do my own will, but the will of Him who sent Me."* (John 6:38)

> *"And He who sent me is with me. The Father has not left me alone, for <u>I always do those things that please Him</u>."* (John 8:29, emphasis added to make the point)

The point is we have the same call and equipment that Jesus had, and therefore we must live up to the higher call of following in His footsteps so the world can see that Jesus is alive, well, and in control of our lives. It is time to become *Genuine* Christians.

The Genuine Christian as an Employee

> *"Servants, be submissive to your masters with all fear, not only to the good and gentle, but also to the harsh. For this is commendable, if because of conscience toward God one endures grief, suffering wrongfully. For what credit is it if, when you are beaten for your faults, you take it patiently? But when you do good and suffer, if you take it patiently, this is commendable before God."* (1Peter 2:18-20)

Christians should be the best employees any employer could ever find, regardless of your field of employment. In 1985, I was still working in the secular world as a Computer Systems Analyst, working with a team responsible for developing computer systems for local county government agencies. Because those I worked with knew I served as a pastor in a small country church, it was obvious I claimed to be a Christian. During this period of my life, the Lord allowed me to witness 1Peter 2:18-20 in action as He led us to be more than hearers but doers of this scripture.

I was a project leader responsible for a team of hard working professionals. I, in turn, reported to a man who was a tyrant and very impatient. He constantly yelled and screamed when anything went wrong that had the slightest possibility of making him look bad. The people were always grumbling and complaining about his leadership style. There were days when some of them would even stay home in order to get even with something the boss said or did the day before. There was strife and confusion constantly in the work place and I was wondering why I had taken that job.

One night, on the way home, I found myself grumbling to God about this man when the Lord spoke these words to my heart. "I want you to teach a Bible study and help those who attend to understand that I expect them to love this man, pray for him, and work harder for him than they have ever worked for anyone." In reply, I argued that I didn't think that was in my job description and, besides, I didn't believe a government agency would approve something like that. The Lord said, "Yes, it is in your job description and yes, they will approve it. You do it and watch what happens!" I knew He meant business and I didn't wish to keep pressing the issue. I decided to see the County Administrator, who is like a company CEO, and ask his thoughts on a Bible study. I figured this way it would be his argument with God, not mine.

The next morning I set up a meeting with the County Administrator. Before the meeting I asked several of my co-workers if they would be interested in attending an after hours Bible study at work. To my surprise, everyone was excited about it. Most of them tried to cushion my feelings by telling me they didn't think I would receive an approval. But as I sat down with the headman, ready to receive a "No", I was totally amazed at his response. "What time of day would you hold this study?" he asked. I told him that we would hold it after normal business hours and that I only needed a room large enough to accommodate around twenty people. He asked, "What are you going to teach?" I told him I hadn't gotten that far yet, but if he would approve a study, I would be happy to share that with him when I figured it out. I couldn't believe it. He approved it right then and there and said, "Let me know what you're going to teach and when you want to start."

On my way back to my desk, stunned with disbelief, the Lord impressed upon me that He wanted me to call the study "*On the Job with Jesus*". As I began to study for this, 1Peter 2:18-23 was one of the first scriptures I studied. To make a longer story shorter, we held the Bible study, which took about eight weeks and we had around forty in attendance on a consistent basis, including the tyrant boss and the county administrator.

It was a little tough on me having my boss and his boss in attendance, but the results were fabulous. People began to apologize privately to the boss after about the fourth week. After the sixth week, I began to receive requests from other employees about topics they would like to study in the future. That in itself was awesome. However, the real impact was the change in the tyrant boss. That poor guy began to calm down and he became almost fun to work with — at least, he was a lot more tolerable.

People in the building who didn't attend the Bible study would ask me, "What have you done with this guy? What in the world is going on with him?" They were all amazed at how he changed and how the staff who reported to him changed. That began a six-year revival in that work place that allowed me to personally lead over two hundred people to a decision for Christ — one at a time. Many in the Bible study also led others to the Lord as well. Several families began to attend our little country church, which brought in a new level of excitement where there had been no excitement for years. That church went from thirty-five on a good Sunday to over two hundred in regular attendance each week. One man who rededicated his life to Christ through all the excitement on the job eventually became my boss and today he is pastor of his own church.

All of this new life occurred because people learned to suffer silently and give their boss the best they had. We all learned through the experiences of those years that being *genuine* is better than grumbling and becoming bitter, religious people who are judgmental and miserable on the job. When you are miserable on the job, it carries over into all aspects of your life. Too many people would use an excuse like that to run to another job rather than to trust the Lord to help them change and become mature, complete lacking nothing. Not only did they change, but they also changed the atmosphere and productivity of the work place. Because of their efforts, they made life better for everyone there. That kind of Christian is able to win others to Christ because, like Jesus, they changed their world.

> *"For to this you were called, because Christ also suffered for us, leaving us an example that you should follow in His steps: Who committed no sin, nor was deceit found in His mouth; who, when He was reviled, did not revile in return; when He suffered, He did not threaten, but committed Himself to Him who judges righteously."*
> (1Peter 2:21-23)

The Genuine Christian's Physical Health

> *"Who Himself bore our sins in His own body on the tree, that we, having died to sins, might live for righteousness — by whose stripes you were healed."* (1Peter 2:24)

I have known Christians who believe that if they say this scripture and others like it, often enough or loud enough they will receive their healing regardless of their lifestyle. I do be lieve that what you say is important when it comes to receiving the promise of divine healing or any other of God's blessings. However saying it, is not as important as doing what the scripture tells us to do and paying attention to what qualifies us to receive the healing. "Well, brother, don't you know that it is your faith in Jesus Christ that qualifies you for His healing power?" Yes, that is partially true. The part most generally ignored is *"...that we, having died to sins, might live for righteousness."* This becomes the most important part and ignoring it will keep you from receiving or keeping any type of divine healing.

Remember, becoming *genuine* means you are faithful to obey

the Lord's Words, spoken as well as printed. Every promise contains a qualifier to which you must pay attention. Ignoring the qualifiers disqualifies you from receiving the promise. *Genuine* Christians are not listeners only, but doers of the Word of God (James 1:22). *Saying it does not replace obeying it* — they must work together for you to reach your goal.

I have also watched as Christians fall into self-condemnation because they could not receive a healing or keep the healing they received. They would beat up on themselves because they had to visit a doctor, take medication, or have an operation.

I firmly believe that *genuine* Christians find peace with God because they follow God's directions. I have received divine healings for my body and I have gone to the doctor as well. I find the faith to receive and keep the divine healings when the Lord speaks a scripture to me. When He gives me a scripture, I stand on it or trust it, until the healing fully manifests.

I talk to God and ask Him what He wants me to do about the health issues of my life. When I have problems, I always ask God for a scripture to stand on as well as, if He wants me to go to my doctor. When He gives me a scripture to stand on and the peace to stand firm, I have the assurance of things hoped for (Hebrews 11:1) and I can stand through anything until my healing comes. When the Lord tells me to go to the doctor, His peace always goes with me and I still have the assurance of things hoped for which gives me the faith to trust my doctor.

Around 1989, I was suffering from infection in my body that completely wore me out, leaving me weak physically as well as emotionally. I was standing on the scriptures the Lord gave me and I fought the infection with my faith for over two years. I also believed the Lord told me to visit my doctor so he could help me fight the infection and find the cause. During this same two-year period, the doctors could not find the cause of this infection, but they did keep me on antibiotics, which probably saved my life. During one of my visits with the doctor, he decided to x-ray my face to see if something was in my sinus cavities. Sure enough, they found a growth in the cavity under my right eye. They wanted to operate immediately and actually remove my face in order to get to the sinus cavity and clean it out. The Lord spoke very gently to me on my way home from the doctor's office. *"Do you trust me?"* He said. I had a sense that the Lord was going to heal me and He did. Several weeks later, I sneezed and guess what came out of my sinus cavity through my nose? You should have seen it! I'll never forget that experience as long as I live. The point I am trying to make is the Lord can use any means He wishes to heal your body — it's up to Him, if He is truly your Lord.

In 2005, I had very high blood pressure with terrible heart palpitations. One day I knew something was wrong; I turned gray, got very light headed, and felt much worse than I looked. I didn't want to go to the doctor because it was in the middle of a very busy schedule. However, my wife would not take no for an answer; rather, she insisted we ask God what He wanted us to do. Thank God she did. We prayed and I asked the Lord if He wanted me to go to the doctor. Immediately I sensed Him saying to me, "GO." That's it. He said Go, so we went. As we were leaving, I asked my wife what she sensed the Lord telling her and she said, "He said GO quickly!" Well, she was driving so we went quickly.

I ended up needing two stints inserted in my heart and one in my renal artery so the blood could flow properly. That saved me, according to the doctors, from having a major heart attack or a stroke. Why didn't God open those arteries for me? I don't have a clue and furthermore it doesn't matter to me. I know He said "Go" and we went and now I am better. I believe that is being *genuine* —listening to God and following the directions He gives us as we go through life.

Being so bull-dog-determined, that God will heal it in a miraculous way and then dying isn't very smart, nor does it bring glory to God. God will never lead us astray or leave us in harm's way, but we need to ask Him what He wants us to do and then obey Him. God knows what you will have the faith for and the Bible says He will never tempt (James 1:13) or test you beyond your ability (1Corinthians 10:13) to grow through it and prosper you spiritually, emotionally, and physically. Remember this, God is the healer, so it doesn't matter if you use the doctors or not. God is the only one who can heal your physical or emotional problems. Doctors can only help control the immediate environment, which helps speed up your healing.

I am afraid many want miracles so they can boast about what great faith they have. *Genuine* Christians just want to be well, physically and emotionally, so they can be about their Heavenly Father's business. Thank God, Jesus bore our sins in His body on a tree, paying for our healing. However, allow God to direct you in how the healing should come. *Genuine* Christians never dictate to God, how something should be done, but humbly work with Him to accomplish His will, His way.

"For you were like sheep going astray, but have now returned to the Shepherd and Overseer of your souls" (1Peter 2:25); this, is being genuine.

It seems that there can be a great deal of physical pain connected directly to our emotional realm. We have seen several people receive the manifestation of their physical healing shortly, if not immediately following the healing of some traumatic memories in their life.

If I am talking to you, please do not despair. Ask the Lord to show you where your body pain or problem began and allow Him to work you though the memories. Just tell Him (verbally) what feels true about you in each memory and listen for His response. When He responds, speak His response out loud [11]and thank Him for showing you the origin. Go through each memory He shows you, in the order He brings them to you. Trust Him and do not question the memories. Hang on to them until you can determine what feels true about you in each memory. If your physical pain does not go away immediately, keep working with the Lord on the memories He shows you. There may be additional memories you need to look at. Besides, several of those we have worked with had their pain go away gradually, over an extended period. Just do not lose hope. God is on your side and He does want to help you. We are the ones who slow things down by dragging our feet when it comes to dealing with our past issues. God is always ready to help when we are willing to go there.

---

[11] For a more complete understanding of why we must repeat what He tells us, refer to Appendix I entitled *Why Must We Speak Audibly To God?*

The Genuine Christian's Relationships

> *"Wives, likewise be submissive to your own husbands, that even if some do not obey the word, they, without a word, may be won by the conduct of their wives. ... Husbands, likewise, dwell with them with understanding, giving honor to the wife as to the weaker vessel, and as being heirs together of the grace of life, that your prayers may not be hindered."* (1Peter 3:1, 7, emphasis added)

We Christians are to live a higher standard within our marriage and family relationships as well. This subject deserves a book of its own.[12] Look at how many books currently make up the *marriage and relationship* shelves in the bookstores. Many ministries operate specifically for that purpose alone. Businesses thrive because of all the materials available for struggling relationships, yet Christian marriages and relationships still suffer and fail in greater number today than ever before. Do you suppose we could be missing something? We are missing something so simple it confounds the wisdom of our age (1Corinthians 1:19).

In our years of ministry, we have seen the *experts* wax eloquent while many times confusing us about how to maintain successful relationships. We have seen too many struggling relationships, literally throw up their hands and quit trying, because no one could help them see what was really going wrong.

I obviously cannot do the relationship subject total justice here. However, I need to touch on it in an attempt to make this book more complete.

We have complicated this whole thing to the point that it is now almost impossible to see how simple God intended it to be. We are relying on human counselors while ignoring the

---

[12] Look for my next book entitled; *Obtaining Marital Bliss* where I teach on the four common causes of communication failures and offer helpful advice for the newly weds as well as those who are fighting to preserve their marriage. Follow its progress on www.ObtainingMaritalBliss.com

Holy Counselor Jesus gave us — the Holy Spirit. After all, His job is to counsel us, lead us and guide us into *all* Truth and righteousness, remind us of *everything* Jesus told us and to tell us *things to come* (John 14:26 and 16:7, 13).

We are working way too hard and it doesn't need to be that way at all. We keep trying to do it or hire it done rather than allow Jesus to fix our problems by giving Him Lordship over our life and our relationships. This is the result of not fully understanding the role of a true Lord.

> *"Seeing then that we have a great High Priest who has passed through the heavens, Jesus the Son of God, let us hold fast our confession."* (Hebrews 4:14, emphasis added)

What is our Christian confession? Is it not that Jesus Christ is our Lord? Romans 10:9 says we must *confess* Jesus Lord and believe in our heart, that God raised Him from the dead to receive salvation. So, what has this got to do with living a higher standard? Let's look at what this section of scripture is teaching us.

Every relationship has tough moments. Every marriage has seemingly impossible times when it seems like the easiest thing to do would be throw in the towel and quit. However, God has prepared His children for these moments by making it possible to enter into His rest. Remember, Hebrews 4:10 says, *"for he who has entered His rest has himself also ceased from his works ..."* The works referred to here have to do with getting even, coping with inner pain, blaming others, running from our pain, etc.

> *"Let us therefore be diligent to enter that rest, lest anyone*

> *fall according to the same example of disobedience."* (Hebrews 4:11 emphasis added)

I would say that throwing in the towel and quitting after you have promised God "*till death do us part*" would be falling, wouldn't you. He goes on to tell us in verse 12 that He has a word for us that is living and active, therapeutic to the point of helping us understand our own thoughts and motives. The only trick is, we need to hear or receive it. He is talking about a word from heaven for the moment. The Lord is talking about a word spoken by the Holy Spirit directly to you, for this exact moment, in your time of need. In verse 13, He continues by explaining that we do not have to explain ourselves or defend ourselves to Him because He sees it all, He understands and He follows in Verse 14 by saying, "*... let us hold fast to our confession.*"

He is saying to hold on to what you confessed for your salvation. Hold on, or continue in your confession and allow Him to be Lord over *all* of your life, the good and the bad — He sees it all anyway. Jesus is asking you to tell Him what you are feeling so He can be Lord over that area of your life. Don't explain it. Just hold fast to your confession. The Lord is saying, *"I've been there, I understand, I know what you are up against. Now come boldly to the throne of grace where I can extend my mercy and supply you with the grace you need for this moment."*

We have watched this work hundreds of times as the people we are ministering to tell the Lord what they are feeling. I have personally experienced this for myself many times down through the years in my journey with the Lord. I certainly expect to experience it many, many more times before He calls me home.

Genuine Christians have found this simple interaction with the Lord as their pathway to peace, freedom, and joy in all their relationships, by becoming *genuine* with God as they live out their confession. This is allowing Jesus to truly be Lord over everything.

I encourage you to pay close attention to the remainder of this book in order to see the simple revelation of becoming *genuine.* As you apply these simple principles to your life your relationships will strengthen, your self-esteem will improve, and your confidence in God and in life will blossom. I have personally experienced it in my life and have witnessed it in hundreds of others who have come to us for help.

Read closely and please do not complicate this book by thinking that our relationship with God will be some mystical, surreal encounter. If you look too deeply, try too hard, or think it is complicated, you are going to miss it and that would be tragic. I believe the Apostle Paul had the same concern for the church at Corinth when he wrote *"But I fear, lest somehow, as the serpent deceived Eve by his craftiness, so your minds may be corrupted from the simplicity that is in Christ Jesus"* (2Corinthians 11:3).

I truly believe that religion, over the centuries, has complicated our view of God, causing us to miss the beauty and power of knowing Him intimately, daily. God did not make knowing Him complex. Man did.

Genuine Christians Live to Bless Others

> *"Finally, all of you be of one mind, having compassion for one another; love as brothers, be tenderhearted, be courteous; not returning evil for evil or reviling for reviling, but on the contrary blessing, knowing that you were called to this, that you may inherit a blessing."* (1 Peter 3:8-9, emphasis added)

Genuine Christians work to become blessings to those around them. They consider other's needs more important than their own (Philippians 2:4). They pray for those who hurt them and spitefully use them and they work to bless those who have cursed them (Luke 6:28). Getting angry and getting even is easy. It takes supernatural strength and ability to walk as Jesus walked.

> *"He who says he abides in Him ought himself also to walk just as He walked."* (1John 2:6)

In his letter to the Church of Philippi, the Apostle Paul taught us how to exchange our anxieties for peace. In nine simple verses, the Holy Spirit, through the pen of Paul, answers the heart's cry of humanity for inner peace with five simple steps. This profoundly simple process has the capability to defeat depression, anxieties of all kinds, phobias, and fears. Let me show you how simple and powerful it is to become a doer of this word.

Step number one is,

> *"Rejoice in the Lord always. Again, I will say rejoice!"* (Philippians 4:4)

This action sets the stage so that good things can take place for the day. If you start out the day grumbling you will more than likely be in much worse shape by bedtime. We can choose how to begin every day. Our choice of how to look at life first thing every morning sets the tone for the total day. We can grumble and complain because it is cloudy and overcast or we can rejoice knowing there is a wonderful, warm sun just behind those clouds and it will eventually shine. I have watched people ruin their entire day just because it is cloudy or rainy. Not only did they ruin their own day, they spoiled the day of everyone they met by making it cloudier inside than it was outside.

Every day in the Lord should be an exciting adventure. The possibilities of our life in God are endless. It is our choice how we live life. Unfortunately, it takes more energy and drive to live it joyfully, purposefully, and positively than it does to live in depression, allowing fears and anxieties to drive you. Too many are looking for a life that takes no energy or drive. They want it easy. The reason it takes more energy is because it creates more life. However, the energy we need to create life and light are all a part of what God supplies when you are connected to Him — the Power Plant of life. Anyone can live in the dark. All you have to do is give up. Living in the dark produces nothing but more darkness. Only mushrooms and mold grow in the dark.

Unfortunately, for too many years I began each day seeing what I did not have rather than rejoicing for what I did have. Rarely was I satisfied with the wonderful life the Lord gave me. I have always had a good home, a great family, and good friends. Rarely have I been in want or need of anything important that I was unable to acquire. When I was actively serving as pastor, my congregation was great as was the vision for the church, and the finances and workers were always sufficient to accomplish the tasks set before us. Rather than purposefully rejoicing in all that the Lord had laid before me I still habitually started each day with my eyes open to the next horizon and what I did not have.

It is good to see the next horizon for the purpose of stretching your faith and keeping you out of apathy. However, when the next horizon (what you do not have) is all you see, each day is no longer an adventure but a torturous experience as you constantly dream and scheme to gain what is just beyond your reach. This mindset, or attitude, makes it impossible to be thankful because, what you have gained and accomplished becomes irrelevant or invisible. A person who can never be thankful, is miserable and dangerously close to losing everything he has. Actually, to say you lose what you have is incorrect because when you are never satisfied with what you have or who you are, you are choosing to squander your blessings on glorifying anxiety and depression, both of which are tools of the enemy. *The enemy is glorified, when you are never satisfied!*

However, Paul's goal was and ours must be, to bring glory

to God, no matter what circumstances we face. Rejoice or revel in your relationship with Him and *choose* to start each day with a smile and a thankful heart to God. It is your choice and your choice sets your attitude. Your attitude powers your actions, and your actions will either prosper you and the Kingdom of God or destroy you while damaging the Kingdom of God and the cause of Christ. Remember; *"Your attitude, not your aptitude, determines your altitude!"*[13]

To rejoice means you choose to see the adventure awaiting you while trusting God to take care of the challenges before you. If you are in a tough spot in life, rejoice for the simple fact that today may be the day of your deliverance. Rejoice because you are in a position to see God's hands work for you. Rejoice, because this is the material that makes good testimonies. It is sad to see all those who can never give God any glory by their testimony. They obviously do not have a testimony, which is a sign that they have rarely, if ever, trusted God to bring them out of a tight spot. REJOICE! Today may just be your day!

One more important thought; if you never allow God the pleasure of bringing you out of a tight spot by His own hand, you will <u>NEVER</u> be able to say, with confidence, *"I can do all*

---

[13] Quote by Zig Ziglar/for more information about changing your attitude, read the author's booklet "Your Pain is Showing" obtainable online @ www.GenuineChristianity.org.

things through Christ who strengthens me" (Philippians 4:13). It is only in the tough spots we experience the strengthening power of God — this is where that confidence in Him is born. REJOICE and be glad for the Lord is at hand!

Step number two is,

"Let your gentleness be known to all men…." Before anyone can see our gentleness, we must get out of our self and do something for others. *When you choose to help others, you will lose track of your own problems.* When you choose to spend your energy in another person's life, you become energized and excited about tomorrow. Sowing your seeds of gentleness and kindness in other's lives today produces the fruit of JOY and excitement tomorrow. That makes the first step of rejoicing easier tomorrow than it was today! Consider this: "RE-JOY-CE". I know it is not spelled correctly, but I hope it makes the point that being joyful is something that is produced by your actions of today so that tomorrow and in all of your future tomorrows, your joy comes easily and naturally. The prefix *re-* in rejoice means to do it again. Do your joy again and again and again until it becomes a habit of life. Reproducing your joy in the Lord is connecting to the Power Plant of life. Re-joy-ce in the Lord every day; I will say it again, rejoice.

It is with a heart of thanksgiving, praise, and being a blessing to others that helps shape our worries into requests or statements to God. There are two ditches on the road of life. One is a ditch of the malcontent. Nothing ever goes right for them. The other ditch is the busy-busy-workaholic-ditch. They are so busy that they never have enough time to enjoy life. In their own minds, no one is as important as those in this ditch are. Communicating with God will keep us in the center of the road. The enemy doesn't care what ditch you are in, as long as you are in a ditch. You become dangerous to him when you are in the middle of the straight and narrow road. Communication with God will give you a heart of thanksgiving. Communication with God will help you become a blessing to others.

Many use their busyness to run from their personal problems. This is as unhealthy as never leaving the *grumpy, malcontent* ditch. In fact, running to keep up with all the good things you are doing may put you back into the *grumpy ditch* because of all you do. Busyness is not always Godliness. God's plan is *not* to make us busy but to make us *responsible* and *effective. Genuine* Christians are responsible and effective, which makes them respond-able to the needs of others and relative to the community and their culture.

Step number three is,

"*The Lord is at hand.*" Rejoice and let your gentleness be known to all. Pressures and trials are a natural part of all interpersonal relationships and life in general. These pressures can cause spiritual and emotional growth, which strengthens the relationships, or they can cause us to become angry, bitter, and envious, losing everything in the end. We cannot be blessings to others if we constantly lose our joy and peace. Expect God to work for you. He is a God of restoration. Be thankful, He is on your side. "*... Work out your own salvation with fear and trembling; for it is God who works in you both to will and to do for His good pleasure*" (Philippians 2:12b, 13).

He is always there and willing to help us work out our difficulties. Working out your own salvation is dealing with the issues that arise from the pressures of life. Many of these pressures could effectively cause you to turn your back on Him and walk away. The Lord has promised us something very important that we often forget. "*I will never leave you or forsake you*" (Hebrews 13:5b). In the original language it is actually, "*I will never, never, never leave you or forsake you.*" God's desire is that we understand that *He is at hand.* He is right here no matter where you are. I thank God that He is alive and actively working in the lives who invite Him. However, unfortunately, if He were dead far too many Christians would never know it or see the difference.

Therefore, rejoice, be thankful, and let your gentleness be known to your loved ones so God can work on all sides of the problem — even on you.

Step number four is,

"Be anxious for nothing, but in everything by prayer and supplication, with thanksgiving..." (Philippians 4:6). This sounds like Jesus in John 14:27, "...let not your heart be troubled, neither let it be afraid." Anxieties are fears and inner turmoil. The fourth point is to make up your mind to quit pretending you are not anxious, by understanding that Jesus has a plan to turn your worry into peace. Jesus told us what to do and Paul is teaching us how to do it. It is easy to obtain the peace of God if you are willing to tell Him about your anxieties.

Step number five is,

Tell God what you feel "*...make your request known to God.*" Don't explain it to Him, but just simply *tell Him.* Many times I fear people look at the words in verse 6; *"...in everything by prayer and supplication..."* and they subconsciously see themselves head bowed, hands folded, on their knees with their halo turned on, praying in all their holiness. It can mean that. However, that picture doesn't fit well when you are in the heat of an argument, dealing with a personal struggle or temptation, at work, or in traffic. Get the picture? And because that religious picture does not fit well with a typical busy schedule we rarely, if ever, give the Lord our anxieties. We just carry them through life. After we have two or three things we are anxious about hanging around our neck, life gets hard because they begin to weigh us down, causing much stress. Is it any reason small difficulties become huge problems with this stuff hanging on us?

> *"Catch us the foxes, the little foxes that spoil the vines, for our vines have tender grapes."* (Song of Solomon 2:15)

Rarely do the big problems ruin the fruit of our life. The *little foxes* get in there and cause our fruit to become bitter. For some reason we seem to handle the big things better — maybe because we expect them or somehow subconsciously anticipate them. But those little foxes seem to get us every time.

God has a much better way. The Apostle Paul is merely telling us that if we *tell God* what we feel, He, God, will send us His peace which, by the way, will surpass all earthly wisdom and understanding as it guards our hearts and minds (soul) through Christ Jesus. No pills or long sessions of telling the counselor everything followed up by human wisdom and more works. No, just *speak* to your Holy Counselor, the Holy Spirit, so He can help you obtain the peace you so desperately need. Sounds simple, doesn't it? Well, it really is. As I have said before, I personally experience it daily and I have helped hundreds of troubled souls find Jesus' peace just this way.

Depression is no match for Jesus if you just tell Him what you are feeling. I don't care if you must tell Him several times a day; He will always have a word for you that will bring you into His perfect peace. There are times when He may say nothing at all, but you suddenly recognize you are no longer concerned and you are even beginning to relax. Years of pain and struggle, washed away by one truthful conversation with the Master.

With these five simple steps, we can chase away the blues and all our fears. It is an antidote for depression, which will only cost you a couple of minutes per session. The good news is that it has "*very low risk of sexual side effects.*" (This is my attempt at being funny; however, it does make a valid and important point.) All joking aside, we have one more responsibility in order to maintain a worry-free, anxiety-free life of peace. We must learn to control the thoughts of our mind.

> "*Finally, brethren, whatever things are true, whatever things are noble, whatever things are just, whatever things are pure, whatever things are lovely, whatever things are of good report, if there is any virtue and if there is anything praiseworthy—meditate on these things.*" (Philippians 4:8)

Many people have very active, powerful minds; powerful in the fact they are constantly thinking and replaying, repeatedly, the things that have happened in their life. They can recall, with excruciating accuracy and clarity, old memories which are painful, those where they think they have failed, where they were hurt by others, or when they were used and abused by life. The minds of these folks can become a proverbial playground for the devil unless they learn how to shut the door and refuse to go there.

Unfortunately, all of us, at one time or another, will battle negative thoughts. If you do not control the power of your mind, it will control you. A mind that is constantly thinking down is a mind pulling its owner into depression. Unless you force your mind to think of good things, it will naturally take you downward. Cases of clinical depression are on the increase in the world today because few are teaching people how to control the thought processes of their mind. (Told to do it, but not taught *how* to do it.)You must take ownership and control of what your mind does and the energy it uses doing it, or you could end up being one of the following statistics.

A report from the National Institute of Mental Health (NIMH) states that, "An estimated 22.1 percent of Americans ages 18 and older—about 1 in 5 adults—suffer from a diagnosable mental disorder in a given year. When compared to the 1998 U.S. Census figures, that translates to 44.3 million people.

Approximately 18.8 million American adults, or about 9.5 percent of the U.S. population age 18 and older in a given year, have a depressive disorder."[14]

What makes these statistics so alarming to me is the fact that the Body of Christ has the answer to this growing problem, yet the problem continues to grow. I must remind the Minister readers that Jesus came to heal the brokenhearted (Isaiah 61:1, Luke 4:18) and He has anointed all of us to minister in the same way (John 20:21).

The mental health professionals cannot heal the depressed, the anxious, or those with compulsive behaviors. They can only teach them how to *cope with* their problems and then they

---

[14] National Institute of Mental Health (NIMH) www.nimh.nih.gov Statistics released in 2001.

medicate them with some wicked mood altering drugs. Once a person is on a chemical maintenance program, very few ever receive medical help to get off the drugs. Doctors do not recommend taking patients off mood-altering drugs for a couple of reasons:

1. The majority of doctors are unaware that emotional pain is healable.
2. The patients themselves do not understand the possibility of freedom from their struggles or the drugs either.

Coping or a lifestyle of maintenance is all they know because it is all they are told. They fully expect to remain on drugs until their bodies cannot take the drugs any longer. As a result, they become increasingly trapped and never healed.

And we wonder why some Christians have a hard time with life? There are issues like this in every church throughout the world. However, unfortunately, the majority of church leadership still thinks the *"expert"'* should take care of people with these problems. Jesus is the healer of the soul, which makes His ministers the experts, but so far, we haven't come to grips with that fact. The church is actually rejecting the brokenhearted and dooming them to a life of imprisonment by not helping them find the healing power of Jesus in the emotional realm.

This is a shame and the shame will fall upon the church because Jesus heals. Right now, He is calling upon us, His body, to love the hurting masses enough to help them get in contact with Him. We, the Body of Christ, must learn to be *ministers of restoration* (Galatians 6:1-3). We must teach them how to work with the Holy Spirit in order to receive freedom from their fears and anxieties. *"Do not let their hearts be troubled. Neither let them be afraid."* (John 14:27, emphasis added.)

How do I know this? Because we have helped hundreds find permanent healing and freedom from life's torments. Many of which were never supposed to be healed, according to their doctors. How have we helped them? By helping them apply the Word of God to their lives (Philippians 4:4-12, Hebrews 4:11-16, 1Peter 5:6-7, etc.). We also help them by facilitating meetings between them and the Lord, as I have tried to describe in this book, so He could speak truth to the painful lies of their mind. We teach people how to be *genuine* and receive from the Lord.[15]

People who constantly fight depression need to constantly do Philippians 4:11 — dwell on good things. It's that simple. We must teach them *how* to take captive every thought and how to bring those thoughts into captivity to the obedience of Christ (2Corinthians 10:5.) We must teach them *how* to have an active relationship with the Living God. They need to be taught *how* to communicate with God — how to become *genuine.*

The problem with this is that it takes more than a couple of Sunday sermons and a Wednesday Bible study to create permanent change in the hurting. Pastor, I am not trying to insult

---

[15]Help and training is available to you on www.GenuineChristianity.org

or condemn. I know your heart for I have been a pastor for over twenty years now. I can sympathize with your overly full schedule. However, the Bible still has the answer — train up the *body* to do the works of ministry (Ephesians 4:12). It has been proven that leaders cannot train anyone to do what they themselves do not know how to do or what they are unwilling to do themselves. The answer to this, as I see it and have experienced it, lies in the following three-step approach:

1. Deal with your own issues. Learn how to gain perfect inner peace yourself and then help your personal family gain the peace of Christ. Become *genuine*. This does not take as long as you may think and you may already be there and not realize it. You may have to rethink your theology a little when it comes to understanding what makes people hurt and do hurtful things. That is one reason for this book and another reason why I want to offer you help. Check it out at www.GenuineChristianity.org. Click on *Seminars* and then *Restoration*.

2. Help those in your congregation, who are looking for help to find release from their torments. The hurting people are there. They have just been quiet, feeling guilty for their pain, trying to fit some unreal view of Christianity. They are waiting for someone to offer them some hope of help. That happens when they hear someone tell them that they are not failures or poor Christians just because they are dealing with some personal issues. They really get ex-

cited when they recognize there is hope and healing for them. When you begin to offer people the *hope of help*, it gives them the permission they feel they need to receive it. This takes some private time with members of your congregation. This is a great time to do some one-on-one discipleship. As they find release from their torments, they will be excited to reach out and help their family and friends.

Aren't we always encouraging our congregations to reach out and help others? I find that when they learn how to get themselves into His peace, they realize they have something to share that works. Suddenly they are excited about reaching others. Suddenly others begin showing up because of what they hear. You will be surprised how quickly the word spreads that there is help available in your church.

3. Train the willing and the mature to minister at this level within the church and their communities.[16] Give them opportunities to exercise their

---

[16] Help is available on www.GenuineChristianity.org Click on 'Resources' and look for R & R Ministry Training (**R**estoration & **R**econciliation **M**inistry).

> gifts and abilities as you oversee them and encourage them to be all they can be in Christ Jesus.

It's time to step up to the plate and take our responsibilities as Christians seriously. It is time to become *genuine.*

Now would be a good time to bring something to your attention. Do you realize that in just five short chapters, Peter, under inspiration of the Holy Spirit, reminds us no less than sixteen times, that life involves suffering, trials, temptations, and struggles? In chapter 4, verses 1 and 2, he tells us to get it into our heads that we had better be ready to go through some things in order to live for the will of God.

> *"Therefore, since Christ suffered for us in the flesh, arm yourselves also with the same mind, for he who has suffered in the flesh has ceased from sin, that he no longer should live the rest of his time in the flesh for the lusts of men, but for the will of God."* (1 Peter 4:1-2)

Now, let's look at the same verses in the Message translation.

> *"Since Jesus went though everything you're going through, and more; learn to think like Him. Think of your sufferings as a weaning from the old sinful habit of always expecting to get your own way. Then you'll be able to live out your days free to pursue what God wants instead of being tyrannized by what you want."* (1Peter 4:1-2, Message Translations)

This takes the veil off and makes it painfully clear, doesn't it?

> *"...For he who has suffered in the flesh has ceased from sin..."* (1Peter 4:1b)

Once you become willing to deal with, and not run from or blame others for, the trials and emotional pains of life, you will see the freedom of maturity that will make you detest the times you ran from them and all the unjust blame you placed on others. Suddenly, you quit demanding your own way and begin to see the value in the struggles life presents. You soon begin to understand why people hurt others and suddenly you find the compassion to help them rising within you rather than the need to judge them. You can then see more clearly that everyone is not out to get you and that the struggles of life can actually become rich blessings to you.

From birth, our common motivation in one way or another is to get our own way. As followers of Jesus, with the desire to reflect His character, that MUST stop. The only way that will happen is to learn the secret of *genuine* Christianity. That secret is *drawing on His strength by and through your verbal communication with Him in every situation.*

> *"My grace is sufficient for you, for my strength is made perfect in weakness."* (2Corinthians 12:9)

The Apostle Paul understood how to be *genuine.* He received the revelation as he personally experienced the Living Christ in his everyday life. In fact, he learned it so well that he was able to go on and say,

> *"Therefore most gladly I will rather boast in my infirmities, that the power of Christ may rest upon me. Therefore, I take pleasure in infirmities, in reproaches, in needs, in persecutions, in distresses, for Christ's sake. For when I am weak, then I am strong."* (2Corinthians 12:10, emphasis added).

That is where we are heading, but it takes one more important ingredient called HUMILITY.

Genuine Christians Serve and Receive from One Another

"Be hospitable to one another without grumbling. As each one has received a gift, minister it to one another as good stewards of the manifold grace of God." (1Peter 4:9-10)

Pride is a wicked thing that keeps us from being *genuine.* Pride that says, "I'm okay! I don't need help. I can do it myself," is just as damning as the pride that says, "I've got the truth and that makes everyone wrong who doesn't agree with me!"

Let's look at this devil called pride for just a minute. The pride that keeps you from admitting you occasionally need help also interferes with those around you by cheating them out of their opportunity to fulfill the Lord's command of *"Love your neighbor as yourself"* (Matthew 22:39). When you ask a brother or sister for their help, you are giving them an opportunity to love you as they serve you. People who think they have it all together needing no help are living in denial in the worst possible way. God did not create you or me to go it alone. God did not intend for us to be "independent," but rather "dependant" upon Him, which will always drive us toward others. Look at 1Peter 4:10 again, *"As each one has received a gift, minister it to one another."*

For every need we have, God has gifted someone close to us to minister his or her gift to that need. The attitude, "I can do it myself," is fear based. It is the fear of "*being exposed*" as possibly incompetent, inadequate, or imperfect. Whatever is driving the fear is stopping you from helping advance the Kingdom of God. You can quote, *"God doesn't give me a spirit of fear..."* (2Timothy 1:7) all you want, but if the fear hangs on, you need to go one-step further. That additional step is to tell the Lord you are afraid and then let Him show you why. He will show you, if, you have faith enough in Him, to allow Him to do it. I have heard people pray and say, *"Perfect Love casts out all fear"* (1John 4:17), but the fear continued to drive them until they gave Perfect Love their fear. Only then, did He drive it out with a word that was living and active (Hebrews 4:12). If you do not give your fear up to Him, He cannot do anything about it. You give it up to Him by telling Him you have it, asking Him to take it.

You may have been applying this to your own life and have found great success with almost everything that has come against you. However, *almost everything* isn't good enough, is it?

This is where you need to have someone who you trust help you.

> *"Confess your trespasses to one another, and pray for one another, that you may be healed. The effective, fervent prayer of a righteous man avails much."* (James 5:16)

The word translated as *trespasses* is from the Greek[17] word *paraptōma*, number 3900 in Strong's. Another valid translation of *paraptōma* is *faults.* "Confess your *faults* to one another." Possibly, you are missing the mark and you do not know exactly why. This is a *paraptōma.* You may have tried time and again to give it over to the Lord, but for some reason you cannot seem to find victory. This is where you need a trusted brother or sister in the Lord to help you.

In Galatians 6:1 the same word is used where it says, "Brother, if a man is overtaken (or caught) in any trespass (paraptōma or fault), you who are spiritual restore such a one in a spirit of gentleness, considering yourself lest you also be

---

[17] All Greek or Hebrew word definitions supplied by "The Hebrew-Greek Key Study Bible" Compiled and edited by Spiros Zodhiates, Th.D. AMG Publishers 1984.

This study Bible utilizes Strong's Dictionary Vocabulary Helps numbering system.

tempted" (my comments added). We are to "Bear one another's burdens and so fulfill the law of Christ" (Galatians 6:2).

If you are hurting, let someone help you, thereby allowing the "law of Christ" to be fulfilled.

"Confess to one another therefore your faults (your slips, your false steps, your offenses, your sins) and pray [also] for one another, that you may be healed and restored [to a spiritual tone of mind and heart]..." (James 5:16 Amplified version).

This process will restore us to a spiritual tone of mind (intellect) and heart (soul). Just what does that mean? When you are hurting or missing the mark and you cannot find victory, you have lost your spiritual tone or fitness. When lies clutter your soul it causes your spiritual condition to be unfit, out of shape, out of tune with God and the Body of Christ in general. Another way of stating this is that your feelings do not line up with your knowledge of how you should be feeling. This creates a psychological conflict which in turn causes behaviors (responses and actions) that are undesirable and difficult to understand.

It happens to all of us in our journey with God. If you believe it hasn't got you yet, you are living in denial. This is caused by *life on a sin filled planet* and Paul is saying, *"Find someone who can help you be restored to the peace that passes all understanding* (Philippians 4:7*), back to God's rest so you don't continue to fall, according to the example of disobedience provided by the Hebrews in the desert"* (Hebrews 4:11). It takes humility to ask for help and that may be the very reason many haven't found the peace for which they are searching. God may be trying to get something out of you called pride. The only way to break pride is to be humbled to the point of breaking.

Before you become *genuine,* you will become familiar with

being broken. If you have never been broken, you will never become *genuine*. Remember, how we relate to one another (horizontal relationships) is indicative of how we will relate to God (vertical relationship). If you cannot receive help from your peers, you are probably not leveling with God either. That is what restoring your spiritual tone of mind and heart means. There is something you believe holding you back and God wants you restored, but sometimes you must seek the help of your brothers and sisters in the Lord to receive it.

The pride that says, "I have the truth and that makes everyone wrong who doesn't agree with me," is the kind of pride that builds walls between individuals and groups. I believe you can take every doctrine to the ditch, and I believe that separating from one another is one of the enemy's tactics to keep you in the ditch. The group you separate from, many times, only wanted to hold you more to the middle of the road. However, promoting your segment of truth seemed more important to you than unifying the body of Christ. Now, I do agree that there are some groups not even on the road. And as Christians, we certainly need to be alert to the basic tenets, or truths of our faith. We cannot compromise them. Here is a worthy saying; "If you do not stand for *something*, you will fall for *anything*." However, there is a lot of foolishness in the Christian community built on pride and fear more than faith.

Anytime we feel we need to separate from members of our own body we need to check to see if it is pride working on us. If it is not pride, you may wish to consider the thought that it could be something inside of you from which you are running or hiding. I have known some to separate and break fellowship because of anger. When confronted they could admit it was anger, but had no idea why. When you face your situation honestly and speak to the Lord concerning your fears, frustrations, and anxieties, you are inviting him to help you and heal you. However, if you run, you will be running forever because wherever you run to you will find the same old problems will be waiting for you when you get there. You might just as well confront it now and get it dealt with so it can't keep you running. Nothing good ever comes when we run from what we should be facing. *Genuine* Christians don't run — they work with God and their brothers and sisters to resolve the issues to build unity and peace.

> *"Blessed are the peacemakers for they shall be called sons of God."* (Matthew 5:9)

If you truly have a revelation or an understanding that others are having a tough time grasping, you need to test it to see if it is of God or just your desire for some level of recognition that will help attract the crowds. First, you can count on other scriptures within the Bible to support any revelation from God. A true revelation from God will make all other scriptures more understandable. A revelation from God will help all who receive it. These revelations that only help certain groups are not from God. The Bible says that God is no respecter of persons (Acts 10:34), so why would God restore a revelation that only affects certain groups and not the entire body? Another truth to consider is that a true revelation of God will help the people of God walk the walk more affectively bringing increased attention to Jesus. And lastly, a true revelation from God will not take anybody back into bondage of the law. On the contrary, true revelation will bring freedom from the curse of the law and perfect inner peace for all. This is what Jesus purchased for us on the cross.

I also believe, however, that this works both ways. Someone

gets a revelation within a denomination or a fellowship group, but the denomination or group leaders cannot or will not consider the revelation (mainly because it was not discovered by them) so they give you the left foot of fellowship. That's considered pride just as much as an individual who will not fellowship with a group because of their different stances concerning their pet doctrines. No matter which way it goes, it's all pride and destructive to the Body and the cause of Christ.

I believe *genuine* Christians will look harder for the common elements that bind us together and then allow God to work out the differences between our pet-doctrines.

> *"Therefore let us, as many as are mature, have this mind; and if in anything you think otherwise* (or differently), *God will reveal even this to you. Nevertheless, to the degree that we have already attained, let us walk by the same rule, let us be of the same mind."* (Philippians 3:15-16, comments added)

Genuine Christians live out what they believe and what God has revealed to them. They are willing to trust God to help those who do not understand, to come to grips with the truth in their own time. *Genuine* Christians will work hard to build bridges and foster love and respect between groups and between individuals. *Genuine* Christians will always extend a helping hand to the hurting, are never fearful of those who are different from themselves, and are always ready to remove the walls erected by pride, prejudices and fear. A *genuine* Christian facilitates healing for those hurting or not complying with "*normal*" Christian behavior in place of casting stones of judgment. In other words, a *genuine* Christian recognizes that hurting people will act in ways unbecoming and many times hurtful. They do not need our judgment; they need our help and understanding.[18] *Genuine* Christians live by the following scripture.

> "*And if anyone thinks that he knows anything, he knows nothing yet as he ought to know.*" (1Corinthians 8:2, emphasis added)

Once we have progressed to the place we can ask for help, not cast judgment, and realize we do not know it all, we are well on our way to becoming *genuine.*

---

[18] Please note Appendix II entitled *Current Failure of today's Church,* concerning a needed paradigm shift in the churches thinking concerning the misbehaviors of Christians and the ability to help them.

Genuine Christians Live a Life of Humility

"The elders who are among you I exhort, I who am a fellow elder and a witness of the sufferings of Christ, and also a partaker of the glory that will be revealed: Shepherd the flock of God which is among you serving as overseers, not by compulsion but willingly, not for dishonest gain but eagerly; nor as being lords over those entrusted to you but being examples to the flock; and when the Chief Shepherd appears, you will receive the crown of glory that does not fade away. Likewise you younger people, submit yourselves to your elders. Yes, all of you be submissive to one another, and <u>be clothed with humility, for God resists the proud, but gives grace to the humble</u>." (1Peter 5:1-5, emphasis added)

Humility is recognizing inwardly and being willing to admit outwardly that we do not know everything yet. It is the inward recognition of our frailties and needs that gives us the strength of character to admit that we need help. This is true with every situation of life as well as with every *feeling* generated by the tough situations of life. The Greek word translated "humble" is *tapeinos*, #5011 in Strong's concordance. One line in the Strong's definition of this word says, "Jesus in His incarnate state in recognizing His absolute dependence upon His Father." Being *genuine* means *reflecting the character and attributes of the founder of our faith*. It also means, *being real*. Jesus said it this way, "*...for without me you can do nothing*" (John 15:5b). The *genuine* Christian recognizes his constant dependency on the Lord. We can do nothing of eternal value without the approval, direction, and power of the Living Christ.

> "*God resists the proud, but gives grace to the humble*" (1Peter 5:5b). The Message translation says it this way. "*God has had it with the proud, but takes delight in just plain people*." (1Peter 5:5b Message Translation, emphasis added)

This is where the rubber of Christianity meets the road of life. This is where we learn the ***how to*** of obtaining all we have been discussing.

> "*Therefore humble yourselves under the mighty hand of God, that He may exalt you in due time, casting all your care upon Him, for He cares for you.*" (1Peter 5:6-7, emphasis added)

I don't know how many times I have heard people pray something like this: "Well, Father, we thank you for your concern for us and we cast our care on you in Jesus' name. Amen." That is *not* casting the care of anything on Him. That is telling Him what He just told us to do.

In order to cast anything on, or give anything to anyone, we must know what it is we are casting or giving. In other words, *what is that care called?* What is its name? In order for God to do something about our cares, we must know what that care is. Generic prayers never accomplish anything. Without identifying just what our care is, we are praying a generic prayer hoping something will stick.

One day I was praying over some stressful things taking place in the church and I found myself saying, "Father, I need your help! Please help me with this situation." I sensed the Lord saying, *"How can I help you?"* Well, I wasn't sure how He could help me I just knew I needed His help. I said, "I don't know! You're God, I just need you." He then said, *"Until you tell me what the problem is, I can't help you."* I had to become more specific about my cares and concerns.

God is definitely aware of and moved by our physical and emotional needs. (Ref. Isaiah 53) However, He is also bound to the laws that govern faith and personal will (Hebrews 11:6). Therefore, He cannot respond to need alone. We know because of the great needs on the earth and the scriptures that it takes faith to move God from compassion to action.

> *"But without faith it is impossible to please Him, for he who comes to God must believe that He is, and that He is a rewarder of those who diligently seek Him."* (Hebrews 11:6)

You must come in faith, with what I call *faith-substance*, and apply it to your particular need, before God has received permission to help us at all. *"Now faith is the substance of things hoped for, the evidence of things not seen."* (Hebrews 11:1) Faith is what levels the playing field for all peoples on earth when it comes to approaching God and working with Him in life. Our faith, or trust in God, expresses our will. It doesn't matter how old or young you are, what color you are, what sex you are. It doesn't matter whether you have extreme beauty or lack it, intelligence or extreme ignorance. It is our *faith in God* that moves God. And for that I say, "Thank you Jesus!" Because, through faith, you and I have the same chances to succeed as Jesus did, or any of the first century Apostles, or any of the Patriarchs the Bible speaks of. In fact, Jesus says it this way.

> *"Most assuredly, I say to you, he who believes in me (faith), the works that I do he will do also, and greater works than these he will do, because I go to My Father."* (John 14:12)

On another occasion while I was in prayer, the Lord impressed upon my mind the following, *"If you cannot admit you have a problem I am not being freed to help you overcome it."* In other words, if we are sick and we can't admit we have a sickness, we have not given God the freedom to heal it. Likewise, if we are unable or unwilling to identify our *cares* or inner turmoil we are not giving God permission or freedom to do anything with them either.

What, then, is a care? Or better yet, how do we identify or name our cares? *Cares always present themselves as BAD FEELINGS.* It's that simple. I know I've said it before, but it bears repeating here; Cares always present themselves as bad feelings. In other words, if you are afraid you are not going to be able to pay all of your bills this month, you are dealing with a care called *fear.* If someone makes you feel like you are a bad person, you are dealing with a care called *guilt or shame.* If something makes you feel *small,* you are dealing with being overwhelmed and that is what you cast onto the Lord. In order to cast that care upon the Lord you would communicate that feeling to Him: "Lord, right now I am feeling rather small or overwhelmed and in Jesus' Name, I ask you to show me why or please take that feeling from me."

> *"And whatever you ask in my name, that I will do, that the Father may be glorified in the son. If you ask anything in My Name, I will do it."* (John 14:13, 14, emphasis added)

Remember earlier when I addressed the renewing of the mind? I said that bad feelings come from believing lies to be true about ones self. All bad feelings need to be paid attention to if we are going to be faithful to Romans 12:2 and complete the transformation or sanctification process that leads us all to becoming *genuine* as followers of Christ.

All bad feelings are an indication that something is wrong. By hiding or running from those bad feelings, otherwise known as coping, we are willingly living in apathy. Apathy is a quiet killer of the church.

> *"Awake, you who sleep, Arise from the dead, and Christ will give you light. See then that you walk circumspectly, not as fools, but as wise, redeeming the time, because the days are evil."* (Ephesians 5:14, 15, 16, emphasis added)

The light this scripture is referring to is the truth. "The entrance of your word gives light; it gives understanding to the simple" (Psalm 119:130). "Your truth is a lamp unto my feet and a light unto my path" (Psalm 119:105).

Far too many people have developed elaborate coping mechanisms that protect them from feeling their emotional pain. Unfortunately, statements we have all heard one time or another like, *"Just get over it,"* or *"Come on, shake it off,"* or *"Get a life,"* or *"If you want to cry, I'll give you a reason to cry,"* or *"You are just way too emotional; get over it,"* have discouraged us from admitting we feel anything. These minimizing comments of frustration, from those who did not know how to help, have emotionally handicapped us all from a very young age. Therefore, we have had to learn how to cope with the pain rather than admit we had it. This coping keeps us from dealing with our painful issues the way God intended.

Many people believe that bad feelings are a sign of weakness. That is a lie in itself. Bad feelings can and do cause us to react improperly which can make us look weak, but the feeling itself is merely helping identify lies about ourselves we believe to be true. Bad feelings are not abnormal or weaknesses anymore than the physical feelings we have when something is wrong inside our body. If it were not for the ability to feel physical pain, many of us would be dead right now. On the same score, many are dying, emotionally and spiritually, because of feelings they are running from or their inability to find someone who can help them find permanent peace.

> *"Be sober, be vigilant; because your adversary the devil walks about like a roaring lion, seeking whom he may devour."* (1Peter 5:18, my emphasis added)

To say, "*whom he may devour,*" indicates that some allow him to devour them. In other words, they are giving him permission. If we do not cooperate with the devil, he cannot devour us. In fact, if we do not cooperate with him and we constantly cooperate with God, the devil must flee (James 4:7) and he cannot even touch us.

> *"...But he who has been born of God keeps himself, and the wicked one does not touch him."* (1John5:18b)

Who in the world would cooperate with the devil? The scripture says it is they who are ignorant of the truth (Hosea 4:6) or unwilling to be humbled under God's hand (1Peter 5:8). As we humble ourselves before God, we are admitting we cannot deal successfully with our feelings alone. As we identify our bad feelings to God, we are casting all our care upon Him because we know He cares for us and He is there to protect us. Those who are running from (or coping with) their bad feelings rather than identifying them and allowing God to speak truth to them are actually working with the devil in their own destruction. Those who are living this way also destroy others as they go down. No one goes down alone. Therefore, if you are running from your feelings, whom are you taking down with you? Think about it!

> *"Resist him, steadfast in the faith, knowing that the same sufferings are experienced by your brotherhood in the world. But may the God of all grace, who called us to His eternal glory by Christ Jesus, after you have suffered a while, perfect, establish, strengthen, and settle you. To Him be the glory...this is the true grace of God in which you stand."* (1Peter 5:9, 10, 11a, 12b).

1Peter 5:9 helped me see that I wasn't the only one suffering. When you are dealing with situations in life that results in having bad feelings it can seem like you are the only one who has ever experienced such a thing. However, the same sufferings are worldwide. It is all part of the human experience. In fact, God uses it to our benefit when we allow Him. Look what the second half of verse 10 says, *"...after you have suffered a while..."* (1Peter 5:10b).

You know how long "*a while*" is. It is as long as it takes you to obey verses 6 and 7. It does not have to be a long time. In fact, I am praying that after reading *Genuine Christianity*, your period of suffering will substantially decrease from what it was prior.

Sadly, I have known people who have suffered most of their lives with feelings that totally held them captive. I am one of those people. For over forty-one years of my life, I suffered with anger. In fact, it was more than anger, it was rage. I had no idea why I was angry all of the time. I just knew that when someone would challenge my decisions or my authority, I would go into a rage that was very destructive. If I tried to fix some inanimate object or machine and failed, I would blow up. When my children were young, I would blow up if they couldn't get along with each other or if they didn't jump when I said to. I was a ticking time bomb waiting to explode. You have probably seen people like that. They are very uncomfortable to be with because they are very easily offended keeping everyone else on edge.

When I was around eleven or twelve my dad revoked my privilege of working in his woodworking shop because I had such an explosive temper. That was devastating to me, as well as to my dad, and I did not blame my dad one little bit. He didn't want to get himself or anyone else in there hurt. After all, we were dealing with power tools, wood, metal, and things that could kill.

People tried to help me by giving me all sorts of advice, such as: "You had better get a grip on yourself before you kill someone or someone kills you." Or, "If you can't act better than that I don't want you around me." Finally, the best one of all; "You had better learn to manage that anger before it gets the best of you." It already had the best of me! Anger management is the biggest joke of all. Emotions are not manageable or controllable; on the contrary, emotions control and drive everything we do.

If you have a hard time with that thought, just begin to pay attention to your actions and you will soon see that everything you do and the way you do or say it will be the result of how you felt at the time. If you feel good, warm, and fuzzy, you cannot say nor do bad things and, conversely, when you feel bad you cannot say nor do good things. You can always be assured that the louder and harsher the profanity, the deeper and sharper the pain.

The good news is God has something better than a management or maintenance program; He has freedom waiting for us.

I did everything anyone suggested. I hit pillows, walls, doors, trees, or anything else that was in the way. I even had a list of nice things I was supposed to say about myself when I got angry. I don't know how anyone can do that one. The doctor put me on sedatives when I was eighteen and told me that if I didn't learn to relax I wouldn't live very long. I had a bleeding ulcer that the sedatives aggravated and I still got angry, so I quit the sedatives. Doctors said they would calm the intensity of my rage. (Talk about an oxymoron. A calm rage — makes me laugh just thinking about it.)

Well-meaning but misinformed Christians informed me that I needed to pray more, so I prayed more. I spent the better part of two years on my face before God, begging Him to take away my anger. Begging does not move God either. Still others said I needed to read more of the Word, so I read more of the

Word. In fact, I memorized the 8th chapter of Romans, with the promise that it would help me live more in the spirit, which it did, and that it would eliminate my rage, which it did not do.[19] I worked and worked and worked at getting control of my anger to no avail, until the day I asked the right person the right question.

I do not desire to discredit any of the advice I received, or those who tried to help me, for I am sure that all of those efforts helped prepare me to receive the answer and the revelation that did set me free. I am only attempting to point out the futility of judging others based upon the obvious misbehavior (sin) of their lives.[20] My desire is to help you get the log out of your eye so you can gently take the speck out of your brothers and sisters eyes. *The church is in dire need of skilled eye surgeons.*

Let's get back to the story. I was in my garage changing the oil in my car and having trouble getting the oil filter off. Whoever put it on before me must have had more ability to reach that thing than I did because it would not budge. And, of course, as my anger built, I naturally thought whoever did this, did it as a part of some evil plot to get me. Everything I tried in

---

[19] For a more complete understanding of the cycle of defeat I was enduring please refer to Appendix II entitled *Current Failure of Today's Church.*

[20] For more on what I see as the failure of the church please refer to Appendix II entitled *Current Failure of Today's Church.*

an attempt to remove that oil filter failed. Well, I finally ruined the filter beyond recognition and I was so furious I came out from under my car and raised my head up too soon and left part of my scalp on the bumper. That was all I could take! I stood in the middle of the floor of my garage and spoke in a very, very loud voice. OK, I yelled. I'm sorry. However, it did teach me that man cannot intimidate God by his outbursts of emotional pain. Nor does it disqualify us from hearing from Him. No, God wasn't upset or frightened at all when I yelled "God, where in the *^#@**%^ is this rage coming from?" The moment I asked that question, I had an instant recollection of an incident that happened when I was nine years old. I had never revisited that memory since the original occurrence. However, when I saw it that day in the garage, I knew what I believed — I was inadequate. As a nine-year-old boy, I interpreted a bad experience I was having, with the lie that said, "No matter how hard I tried I would not be good enough!"

The moment I saw that memory it made me feel so terrible that I spoke to God in the same very loud voice "It looks like I've been inadequate all of my life!" The most wonderful thing happened to me at that moment; God spoke back to me and said *"I have never made anyone or anything inadequate. When you find your purpose you will also find how adequate you are."* I was so shocked to receive that from God that I said to Him "Did you just say I am not inadequate?", thinking I was going to press my argument to convince Him that He must have made a mistake with me. The moment I spoke those words out of my mouth the greatest peace settled over my entire being. I could not explain this sudden rush of peace. Philippians 4:7 calls it the *Peace of God that passes all understanding*. Hebrews 4:12 calls it a *living word, sharper than any two edged sword.* James 1:21 calls it *the implanted word, which is able to save your soul.* And Jesus teaches in

John 17:17 it is *sanctification by truth.*

I could feel all the years of pent up poison drain from my soul as I meditated on those words. I felt the presence of God wash over me physically and spiritually. I was experiencing a *transformation* (Romans 12:2b) so spectacular I could hardly believe it was happening to me. I was experiencing *"the purification of my soul in obeying the Truth"* (1Peter 1:22). The Truth Jesus spoke to me, totally washed away the feelings of inadequacy that had been covered and protected by my anger. I had just experienced John 8:32. *"And you shall know the Truth and the Truth shall make you free."* Free from over forty-one years of miserable anger and rage that worked to destroy my life. The feelings that caused that anger [fear and inadequacy] made me physically sick and worse yet, it made me a workaholic, an alcoholic, and an all around miserable human being. In a matter of seconds Jesus took it all away because I asked Him the right question and, unknowingly at the time, put my faith in what He said by speaking His response back to Him. As God and my wife are my witnesses, my *sin* called *rage* left me that moment and I have been free ever since. It has been many years now since I was constantly fighting with my sin. I cannot even find any pain or discomfort in that memory now. It is now just a fond childhood memory.

> *"Therefore, if the Son makes you free, you are free indeed"* (John 8:36). Thank you Jesus!

Please study Appendix I *"Why We Must Speak Audibly to God"* to more fully understand the benefits of a verbal relationship with God. However, for now, I wish to draw your attention back to 1Peter 5:10b, *"...after you have suffered a while...."* A while for me was forty-one years. In a matter of seconds, Jesus did what no one else could do: He healed me and brought me into His perfect peace, destroying the cause of my sin. Every time we take our bad feelings (cares) to God, He has promised us something important to which we need to pay attention. Look closely at this verse.

> *"But may the God of all grace, who called us to His eternal glory after you have suffered a while, perfect, establish, strengthen and settle you."* (1Peter 5:10b, emphasis added)

He promises to perfect you or *mature* you as well as to establish you. To establish you means to *set you on a solid rock foundation* that will never give way under you. He also promises to strengthen you. This is an *inner strength* that is both emotional and spiritual. This is where our confidence in God comes from — our inner strength (Isaiah 32:17). He also promises to *settle you,* which paints a picture of a contented flock of sheep, *quietly resting* in green pastures beside still waters. He brings you into that quiet, peaceful rest for which everyone is dreaming and into which God has called us.

With every feeling (care) we take to God we gain a greater portion of His perfect peace. Our faith in Him becomes more solid and real (*genuine*), we quit fearing our feelings, and we quit blaming others for them. This is maturity! This is the transformation promised us in Romans 12:2 and the sanctification that continues everyday of our lives in this natural body.

After receiving our promised reward, by trusting Jesus with our feelings of life, Peter adds; *"... this is the true grace of God in which you stand"* (1Peter 5:12b, emphasis added).

True Grace is another way of saying "*Genuine Christianity*". This, my friend, is how to become g*enuine* in your faith.

We will stand by the power of His true grace only when we work with God to become *GENUINE Christians.*

"Now acquaint yourself with Him, and be at peace;
Thereby good will come to you.
Receive, please, instruction from His mouth,
And lay up His words in your heart.
If you return to the Almighty,
You will be built up;
You will remove iniquity far from your tents.
Then you will lay your gold in the dust,
And the gold of Ophir among the stones of the brooks.
Yes, the Almighty will be your gold and your precious silver;
For then you will have your delight in the Almighty,
And lift up your face to God.
You will make your prayer to Him,
He will hear you, and you will pay your vows.
You will also declare a thing,
And it will be established for you;
So light will shine on your ways.
When they cast you down, and you say, 'Exaltation will come!'
Then He will save the humble person.
He will even deliver one who is not innocent;
Yes, he will be delivered by the purity of your hands."
Job 22:21-30

Freedom Means You Are Free to Choose

"And you shall know the truth, and the truth shall make you free." (John 8:32)

"For the law of the Spirit of life in Christ Jesus has made me free from the law of sin and death." (Romans 8:2)

One of the beautiful qualities of the Lord is that He will never alter your will for His or anyone else's convenience. His desire is that all human wills line up with His will, which is the only source of total goodness. However, He will never force you to change your will. Your will determines your ultimate actions. You will always have total control of your will and your resulting actions unless, of course, you give that control to someone else. Even then, you are ultimately responsible for your own actions.

Your will is not something given to you as a part of God's

creation, but something that life has helped or forced you to develop. Your will is what you choose to do with what is in your soul and heart. Our will can change, thank God. What causes us to change our will for good or bad are the feelings and knowledge stored in our mind from our life experiences.

It is important to understand that healing your wounded emotional past will not automatically alter how you ultimately act or respond in the future, given similar circumstances. You must choose how you respond in every circumstance of life. Eliminating the lies in your mind reduces or eliminates the force outside of your control that caused your behavior to be unacceptable. However, you will still be responsible to choose the course of your life, moment by moment.

We have worked with many, brought to us by others with high hopes that we could help them find a new level of peace that would alter their behavior. Even though they were hurting terribly, those suffering did not choose to come on their own. A well-meaning parent, relative, friend, or pastor made the decision for them because of some behavior pattern that was unacceptable. Therefore, the well-meaning person was, unknowingly and unintentionally, trying to change the hurting person's will. In the case of a parent seeking help for a child, the child has no control over the decisions made for them so they merely go along for the ride, so to speak. However, in the case of a friend, relative, or pastor seeking help for another, many times the person hurting is afraid of disappointing the one trying to help, so they just go along for the ride as well. Results in these cases are usually very disappointing to the ones trying to help. Why? Because being changed or healed was not, in these cases, the will of the one hurting.

The person whose behavior is unacceptable is the one who must make the determination to seek help before help of any kind can be effective. You can jump through all the hoops, say the right words, and play along, and even get some healing along the way, but, if your will never changes, your behavior will never change. If your behavior never changes, Christ gets no glory. If Christ gets no glory from your life you are fooling no one but yourself; your will needs to change. Your will begins to change when *you* decide your behavior is unacceptable and *you* make the move to seek help. When this happens, we have seen God heal some serious and long running difficulties. I am constantly amazed at how the Lord heals and changes a person's life, including my own.

For those of you who may desire to help others, remember, the hurting person is never happy with themselves or their behavior. They hate what they do and how they feel about their actions. They also hate what their behavior ultimately makes them feel about themselves. Therefore, the way to help them become willing to seek help is by informing them that when they get tired of *feeling what they feel*, there is help and healing available to them. Tell them that you care for them and understand how miserable they must be: Please remember however, there is nothing you can do to help them, until they decide, on their own, to receive help. When they make that decision, they will receive help! This is not condemning, but hopeful. When people feel a sense of hope without the condemnation that comes from the thought that they need to "get fixed", they usually come around much quicker.

Once you have received release from the lies and your feelings about life have changed, you suddenly recognize that you at last have a choice of how to respond. After I received the healing from feelings of inadequacy, I remember clearly the first opportunity I had to live in my newfound freedom, or to resort to an old, well-established habit. My response to feelings of inadequacy had been anger, resulting in instant rage for over forty-one years. You can build a strong habit in forty-one years of triggered responses. Therefore, as I encountered my first life situation, that would have originally sent me over the edge before I received the truth; I knew I had to make a choice. I clearly recognized my feelings were not as they had been. I knew I was free from being triggered into rage, which I hated all along but did not know how to escape. Suddenly, in a split-second flash, I recognized I was free to choose and therefore, I chose to respond in a more appropriate manner, rejoicing in my newfound freedom.

I have worked with some who received wonderful change but refused to make the choice to respond in an appropriate manner. After you receive the truth that changes what you are feeling, *you* are then *responsible* for your actions. Prior to receiving the truth, your behavior or responses were triggered reactions you had little to no control over. Therefore, you are not guilty of what you have no control over. However, after receiving the truth, you are free or capable to choose; therefore, you must choose to respond in an appropriate, godly manner. *Genuine* Christians will always choose to respond as God leads them by listening for His instructions and obeying Him. Once your soul has been purified (1Peter 1:22) you are free, capable, and responsible to listen to Him and respond as He instructs you. After Jesus gives you the truth, you are then responsible for your reactions. *Genuine* Christians gladly accept that responsibility.

This is when it is very important to cognitively know the written Word of God. The Spirit of God will never tell you to do anything that is contrary to the Bible. He will never cause you to do anything outside your realm of control. He will never cause you to respond hastily or rudely. Knowing the written Word of God helps you determine if what you are hearing is from God or from yourself and your human desires. Our human desires can sound a lot like God sometimes.

Many times the Spirit of God will say nothing because you already know what the Word of God is telling you. For instance, when I get angry I know it is inappropriate to go into a rage, not because I hear the voice of God every time, but because I know what the word of God teaches.

> *"Be angry, and do not sin: do not let the sun go down on your wrath, nor give place to the devil."* (Ephesians 4:26, 27, emphasis added)

In other words, because of my cognitive knowledge of the written word of God, I know that anger is not a sin, but how I choose to respond could be. To deal with my anger properly I must face it, deal with it immediately, and respond in a godly manner before I have completed and managed my responsibility properly.

Without a good base knowledge of the written Word of God, you are going to have problems in life, regardless of your emotional pain. We need a balance to be healthy spiritually as well as emotionally. That balance is called being *genuine*. Listening to the spirit only, with no knowledge of the written Word of God, will put you into the devil's playground where you can expect to be in trouble most of the time. Conversely, if all you have is your knowledge of the written Word of God, never listening to the Holy Spirit, you will become religious, dry, lifeless, and powerless. The Bible teaches that knowledge alone puffs us up (1Corinthians 8:1b), and the Holy Spirit gives us life (2Corinthians 3:6b), and power (Acts 1:8); therefore, do not become a puffy, lifeless, powerless Christian. Be balanced, be *genuine*, and be real.

Another saying I like along these lines that may help you is, "All spirit and no word will cause you to blow up; all word and no Spirit will cause you to dry up; but the Spirit and knowledge of the word will cause you to grow up."

Balance brings spiritual maturity or, *genuine* Christianity.

Appendix I

Why Must We Speak Audibly To God

Because we insist that people we are helping speak audibly to God, they generally voice some concern. Their main concern, it seems, comes from these three basic questions. 1) How do I know if what I am sensing is from my mind or from God? 2) How do I know if what I hear is from God or the devil? And 3) what is the biblical support for this bizarre request?

I will address this issue from those three questions.

> 1) How do I know if what I am sensing is from my mind or from God?

Something dynamic happens when you speak audibly what you sense God saying to you. As you begin to speak what you sensed, it just feels right if it was from God. If it was a product of your thought process, it will not feel quite right. You will just know where it was from if you speak it so your ears can hear it. If you sense it was from your thinking, and we will all miss it occasionally, just ask God to forgive you, quiet your mind, and ask Him to please speak to you again. Don't get the foolish notion that if you miss it the first time God will not speak it again. No, He is patient with us and He understands how noisy it is here. However, if you just don't like His answer and you refuse to obey, do not ask Him again hoping He will change His mind. Forget it. He will not speak it again. God knows when we are earnestly and honestly attempting to communicate with Him. He also knows when we are playing our little games.

When you speak what God is telling you, *it will change you and you will feel it.* If you speak what your mind was thinking, it will not have any changing effect on you. In fact, much of what your mind will be thinking will probably be negative. What comes to us from Heaven is always peace loving, gentle, patient, encouraging, etc. (James 3:17). Never forget, this is a faith walk. We cannot please God without faith and communicating with Him is a great place to exercise your faith.

2) How do I know if what I hear is from God or the devil?

I answer this one first with a question: "Who were you talking to?" If you asked *me* a question, wouldn't you expect *me* to answer it? If you are asking God a question, don't you think He is big enough to answer it? The Bible teaches us that if we are submitting to God, the devil will flee (James 4:7). You cannot submit to God and to the devil at the same time. Speaking to God and expecting the devil to answer is called being double-minded. Also, James teaches us that because he is double-minded he should not think he will get anything from God. *"If any of you lacks wisdom, let him ask of God, who gives to all liberally and without reproach, and it will be given to him. But let him ask in faith, with no doubting, for he who doubts is like a wave of the sea driven and tossed by the wind. For let not that man suppose that he will receive anything from the Lord; he is a double-minded man, unstable in all his ways"* (James 1:5-8, emphasis added).

Next, let's look at what Jesus said about our communicating with Him: "And when he brings out his own sheep, he goes before them; and the sheep follow him, for they know his voice. Yet they will by no means follow a stranger, but will flee from him, for they do not know the voice of strangers" (John 10:4, 5, emphasis added).

Asking the question "Will it be God or the devil?" is really saying, "I have more fear of the devil than I have faith in God's ability and desire to communicate with me." When stated that way it sounds bad, but isn't that what it is really saying? Come on; let's give God more credit than that. Start exercising your faith in God's promises rather than your fears.

We have access to all the wisdom of heaven; we have the mind of Christ, if we access it. If we do not ask, we will not receive. If we constantly doubt God's ability and desire to answer us, we are without hope. Talk to God audibly, respond to God audibly, and watch how dynamic your relationship becomes.

3) What is the biblical support for this bizarre request?

In addition to what I have already given you, look at Isaiah 55:11. "So shall My word be that goes forth from My mouth; It shall not return to Me void, but it shall accomplish what I please, and it shall prosper in the thing for which I sent it."

Throughout teaching this process of building and maintaining a relationship with God, I have tried to make clear the understanding that having a relationship with the Divine works like any successful relationship with any mortal here on earth. Without verbal communication, you have no relationship.

Let's look at the beginning of our relationship with God. Romans 10:9 teach that "*if you confess with your mouth the Lord Jesus and believe in your heart that God raised Jesus from the dead, you are saved.*" In other words, your relationship must begin with you speaking to Him. You cannot *think* Jesus is Lord and be saved. The scripture is very clear; you must *confess* Jesus is Lord before any relationship can begin. Without speaking audibly, you are not speaking.

If God does not speak to you concerning your issues, you will not find release from them. Likewise, if you do not speak to God what He speaks to you, you will not find any release either. In Isaiah 55:11, He tells us that His word will not *return* to Him void, or empty of power. Therefore, we are responsible to put the power in what He speaks to us. Here is how it works.

Everything God does, He does in a Divine order called a life cycle. Things come from heaven to accomplish something on the earth so it can return to heaven. For instance the rain and snow comes from heaven to water the earth causing the earth to give forth plants for our benefit (Isaiah 55:10). The plants absorb the moisture from heaven and take from it the nutrients gathered in the atmosphere and soil, which feeds the plants and then, through evaporation, releases the moisture back into the atmosphere through the leaves, making a complete life cycle. This is a very simple explanation; however, everything God does is in this order. Jesus came from heaven to earth, completed His work on the earth, and then returned to heaven. Therefore, everything that comes from heaven must return to heaven to complete the cycle. If the cycle, or order, is broken, you will not receive the results expected. Everything God speaks is to produce something on the earth. As this happens through us glory and praise return to God.

Think about the many wonderful ideas God has sent to man that could have benefited mankind, but instead went to the grave with the person God wanted to produce it through, all because they did nothing with the idea. *You will never do anything that you do not speak about first.* In speaking, your faith is increased.

Look at the Divine power that is in our control. Jesus taught us something very important that we need to remember. "... *For out of the abundance of the heart the mouth speaks.* (Matthew 12:34b).

The word translated *heart* is taken from the Greek word *kardia;* #2588 in Strong's. The Strong's definition is: "thoughts, reasoning's, understanding, will, judgment, designs, affections, love, hatred, fear, joy, sorrow and anger since these things can actually affect a man's physical heart. Therefore, the heart is used for the mind in general." *This is the place where all your experiences, education and passion meet. This is where the source of your character is stored. Your heart,* ***kardia,*** *is where your gut feelings reside.*

In other words, *kardia* is referring to the center of your very being. We do not speak what we do not believe. What we speak identifies where our faith is.

Therefore, when we sense we have received something from God, we must complete the cycle by putting our faith in it and sending it back to God. How does His word return to Him? By our releasing it through our mouths as we speak it. We are putting our faith (power) into the containers (words) God sent us and then sending them back to Him, filled with power, as we speak them, which releases God to accomplish what He sent them forth to do — create life by making us free

(John 8:32). When we do not speak forth what He speaks to us, we do not complete the cycle, thereby stopping God from helping us.

What about the mutes who cannot speak? If your attitude is to release your faith so God is free to work for you and you communicate by sign language, I know God understands sign language. You can write your responses or use unintelligible groaning and God will still respond to you because God understands your heart. No physical handicap will stop God or handicap Him. He only needs our indication that we have enough faith in what He said to us to offer our communication to Him in whatever ways we have learned to do that.

Over the years, we have helped hundreds of people receive perfect peace by teaching them to speak what God has told them. During these experiences, we have had several who, when they see a memory and hear from God, would get a disgusted look on their face but say nothing. When I asked them, "What did the Lord say?" they would often shrug and say, "Oh, just the same thing I have heard before." I would have to press the point with them and in a few cases I can remember, I would almost have to force them to speak what it is they sensed the Lord tell them. However, when I finally convinced them to speak it out loud, they always received the peace or change for which they were searching. They never received the physical manifestation they needed because they never spoke what God had been telling them all along.

I believe that the Lord is quite often speaking to us, but if we refuse to speak out loud or respond to Him about what He says to us, His words will do us no good. How terribly much pain and confusion the Body puts up with just because we refuse to walk by faith and speak out loud what we sense Him speaking to us. I must agree with Joseph Scriven when he wrote, "*Oh, what peace we often forfeit, O what need-less pain we bear, all because we do not carry everything to God in prayer.*

Appendix II

The Current Failure of Today's Church

First, please understand that I love the church — the Body of Christ. I love everything it stands for and has the capability of being. I have great hopes of personally seeing the Glorious Church the Apostle Paul mentioned in the book of Ephesians. The church, as with a perfect bride, is to be without spot or wrinkle and holy and without blemish (Ephesians 5:27). I personally believe that is Jesus' and the Holy Spirit's current ministry to the church — washing us with the water of the Word in order to present us perfect (mature) and blemish free: To *reveal* and *restore* truths that were long ago stolen from us or simply forgotten through easier, less stressful times. The world needs this type of church with the power and the peace it will provide all who enter. However, we are a ways from that today and that alone should concern all of us enough to cause us to search for answers. I also believe that it is our responsibility to inform the Body of errors discovered that are currently destroying this awesome potential. It would be much simpler for me to go about my business hoping everyone else gets it before long. However, that is not what God is calling me to do.

My purpose for this appendix is to humbly offer information, gained through years of personal and professional experiences, that is currently correcting this error in individual's and their churches. By correcting the error we get closer to becoming the Glorious church without spot or wrinkle, elevating the church back to a relevant source of moral activism as well as a resting, healing place from the storms of life for those who desire to enter.

The Error

Unfortunately, much of the church still believes that true freedom is living without sin. *The freedom that Jesus died for is the ability to live in truth!* (John 14:27) Trying to live without sin is an impossible and self-defeating process. This process creates *legalism* and *hypocrisy*. Jesus referred to it as trying to be perfect on the outside while ignoring all that is taking place on the inside (Luke 11:39). Being sin-conscious *causes* sin in those who's sin nature was circumcised (Romans 6:6-7, Colossians 2:11). Being sin-conscious gives sin power over us by the fear it creates. When you allow fear in your life, you give power to that which is causing the fear. The power of sin that Jesus died to destroy, regains its power and therefore, its control by our being sin-conscious.

Being able to live in Truth, or in Christ, is not concentrating on sin at all. Living in Truth, or abiding in Christ, brings the understanding that when you lose your peace (John 14:27) (Which causes you to sin.) a lie hidden in your soul is being exposed. By looking to God to replace the lie with His truth, your emotional pain leaves with the lie; stripping sin of all the power that it once held over you (Romans 6:7).

In my personal experience and my professional experience of ministering to hundreds of troubled Christians, the sin within the church is not the root problem; it is the *fruit* of the real problem, which is the *lie* believed to be true by the one struggling. Knowing that believing a lie is the cause of emotional pain helps us understand why we do, at times, what we really hate to do (Romans 7:15, 19). It also makes the misbehaviors of others around us less threatening to us personally. Recognizing the source of other's misbehaviors gives us more understanding and empathy for our brothers and sisters. This understanding alone brings more peace to the local church and eventually the Body of Christ universal.

We humans are unable to control our feelings; on the contrary, our feelings control us. So, in effect, the sin is not causing us all our pain, but our root *pain is causing us to sin.* I am not saying that sin does not cause pain. Sin does cause pain. I am saying, however, that the sin *Christians* find themselves in only increases the pain that drove them to the sin in the first place. For example, being an alcoholic is not the real problem; it is the fruit of the problem. The real problem (or root) is the *pain* from which the alcoholic is trying to hide. Help an alcoholic or drug addict, homosexual, abuser, gambler or any other person who is sinning eliminate the pain and the sin will usually cease. Once you have identified and dealt with the root problem, the once hurting individuals must then learn Godly ways of responding and reacting to life. When the pain disappears, those once hurting can now pay attention and learn how to live Godly. Trying to teach a person in pain how to live above the pain is like shouting swimming lessons from the shore to a drowning person. It doesn't work very well. We have been blessed to help many Christians trapped in one or more of these sins find true, permanent freedom. True *rehabilitation* only comes from God. Sinful behavior, in the life of a Christian, is a hiding place from, or a coping mechanism for, emotional pain.

If you believe, as many in the church do, that a Christian's sin or bad behavior is the only cause of their emotional pain, then you also believe that the act of confession and repentance are the only and complete answers.

> *"If we confess our sins, He is faithful and just to forgive us our sins and to cleanse us from all unrighteousness."* (1John 1:9)

It is true, Jesus does forgive us and cleanses us from all unrighteousness when we recognize we missed the mark and are willing to confess it to Him. However, cleansing us from the results of our actions or words and healing us from the cause of our sin are two different things. The Roman Catholic Church has a very long history of trying to cause a change of behavior by mandating confession for healing. It does not work — ask all the Priests caught and charged with improper behavior, if all their time confessing their sin actually took away the cause of their sinful behavior. The Protestant Church has the same problems going on within it as well. No one group has a corner on ungodly behavior. My hope and purpose for this section, as I have said before, is to help in reducing the error by sharing what I have experienced that works. I am not talking about working once or twice, but hundreds of times since 1999. We have spent thousands of hours in fulltime ministry to emotionally hurting Christians and non-Christians alike from around the world. It works every time.

I thank God that, during my personal battle with rage, I was able to find moments of *temporary relief* from this cycle of destruction. That temporary relief amounted to me confessing to

God that I was a weak sinful creature who, in my own mind, did not deserve His love because I could not get a grip on my anger. I actually had a well-meaning Christian leader tell me that the way I was confessing was my problem. Therefore, desperate to find permanent healing, I changed my methods of confessing, the tone of my voice and the length of my confession. I even tried taking communion when I was confessing, but none of these techniques improved my ability to control my rage or lengthened the times between my outbursts. Following is a picture of what my cycle of behavior looked like.

1. Something would trigger my rage and I would **EXPLODE!**

2. Guilt and self-condemnation would set in as soon as I ran out of energy and collapsed in a pile of tears and regrets. (Romans 8:1 made me feel even guiltier.)

3. Depression would set in for a period—usually for a couple of days.

4. I would finally break before God and in tears confess my sin and repent and promise Him I would *try harder* next time, which, is what I was told I needed to do.

5. I would find His soothing touch calming and the reassurance that He loved me very helpful until something would trigger my rage and the cycle would start all over again.

With each pass through that cycle, I would lose: confidence in me as a Christian, the excitement and joy received during my good days, my hope of ever amounting to anything as a Christian. Worst of all I lost my confidence in God's ability and willingness to put up with me and deliver me. It is like digging your own grave, burring yourself in the shame and guilt of not being good enough to make it.

Thank God, I did get free from that cycle of self-defeating works. However, many Christians are in the same self-defeating cycle of despair. Despair caused by their belief that our misbehavior is the cause of our pain and if you can't find relief through repentance and trying harder, something unredeemable must be wrong with you. That is not what anyone said to me. However, that is the feeling and impression received, as many of today's Christians attempt to find permanent freedom while struggling with their improper behaviors.

I am here to tell you there is NOTHING Jesus cannot heal or NO ONE Jesus cannot redeem. Nothing is greater than He is, but we must first learn how to work with Him to affect peace in hurting minds. It is time the church begins to help heal the brokenhearted and open the prison doors to them bound in dungeons of self-defeat. By not helping, we are causing more guilt and shame by judging them as rebellious sinners who are not paying attention.

You can pick bad fruit all day long and never destroy the root that caused the fruit in the first place. That is what I was doing as I worked to manage or control my sin known as rage. That is what I am afraid the church is doing. It's time we quit picking the bad fruit and get to the root of our misbehaviors caused by our pain and despair.

The church needs a slight paradigm shift of thinking when it comes to helping those whose presentation and maturity level is less than desirable.

To arrange speaking engagements, seminars or R&R Ministry Training sessions (Restoration & Reconciliation), ask questions, or to obtain other teachings and writings of the author please feel free to

Contact us through the following addresses:

www.GenuineChristianity.org
or
www.GenuineChristian.org

Appendix III

All to the Glory of God

"Praise is awaiting You, O God, in Zion;
And to You the vow shall be performed.
O You who hear prayer, To You all flesh will come.
Iniquities prevail against me; As for our transgressions,
You will provide atonement for them.
Blessed is the man You choose, And cause to approach You,
That he may dwell in Your courts.
We shall be satisfied with the goodness of Your house, of your holy temple.
By awesome deeds in righteousness You will answer us ..."
Psalm 65:1-5

In the following testimonies, you will hear how God has always healed the hurting, broken hearts of all who dare approach Him. I have heard some say that God does not have the time to concern Himself with our petty problems. *There has been no lie perpetrated upon this hurting world greater than this!* God is ever present, ever ready, and willing to touch anyone who will come with the faith to address Him. How it must make God weep that His body, the church, is so calloused to the cry of, or fearful of the hurting that few have the confidence to say, "Come, for I know He will heal you and give you peace." My prayer is for that condition to change quickly.

You will be hearing from the professional businessman, the student, members of the clergy, and the layman. You will hear from the housewife, career woman, the rich and the poor. For all of mankind, regardless of their position in life, have hurts that only God can heal. All are suffering from inner turmoil and fears that shorten lives, weakens relationships, and destroys families and churches. All are healable and only a conversation or two away from total inner peace. My prayer is that these testimonies encourage and inspire you to step out of your comfort zone and seek help so that *you* can begin to help the hurting.

Each testimony is written in the person's own words; however, their names and locations have been omitted to protect their privacy. Their testimonies are included to bring glory to God only and not to solicit anything. However, if you need help, I would not discourage you from contacting us as we know of other restoration ministries and one may be close to you.

For the purpose of encouraging the hurting and educating the church only, I mention the following types of conditions that we have seen healed and, in many cases, totally released from other types of care.

- Addictive and compulsive behaviors
- Abuse victims, physical as well as emotional abuse
- Depression
- Eating Disorders
- Grief/Loss
- Fears and Phobias of all kinds

- Substance Abuse
- Post Traumatic Stress Syndrome/Disorder (PTSD)
- Sexual Dysfunctions such as addictions, homosexuality, frigidity

I know it may be unbelievable to some of you, but all of these terrible conditions are in the church. Any one of these conditions may be sitting next to you next Sunday. That is why it is so important for the Christians to wake up and prepare to help the hurting. This is not something outside of the church. These are our brothers and sisters in the Lord and they need freedom and not condemnation.

To those suffering with one or more of these conditions, be blessed and be hopeful. God is in favor of YOU! God is on your side!

Appendix IV

Testimonies to God's Glory and Grace

Dear ministers at Master's Touch;

I came to you a battered and confused young lady. My worst enemy was myself due to the events of my childhood. When I was young, several males sexually abused me over a long span of time, eight to twelve years. Because of this, I had a general distrust and hatred of men. I felt that I wasn't worthy of anything that was good because I blamed myself. Most of all, I was afraid of any future sexual experience and yet I really wanted to get married and have children.

I met with ministers at Master's Touch and through several sessions of digging out the roots and allowing Jesus to speak truth to me I have found so much freedom! At the time, the sessions were very difficult for me because I was so buried in lies that I was afraid of the truth. Each time I found more freedom and less fear. Eventually, I was a completely changed person.

I can happily say that I have much more self-esteem now and I do not constantly put myself down and declare that I am fat. Most importantly, at least in my eyes, I have found a wonderful man who loves me and whom I love. We are to be married next month and for the first time in my life, I am not afraid of a man. Neither am I afraid of the wedding night. Sex is no longer a bad or frightening word for me. I am free from fear and life is wonderful!

Thank you so much.

I will praise You, O Lord, with
My whole heart;
I will tell of all your marvelous
works.
I will be glad and rejoice in You;
I will sing praise to Your name,
O Most High.
Psalm 9:1, 2

Dear ministers;

It seems incredible that Jesus can truly restore years of time seemingly wasted in prisons of our own making. Such a bittersweet process to experience the depth of His grace running parallel to a sudden revelation of our own deception. Seems like a bunch has happened since that day.

Thank you—I love you guys.

And those who know Your
Name will put their trust in You;
For You, Lord, have not
forsaken those who seek You.
Psalm 9:10

From childhood through my adult life I had been abused

mentally, physically, and emotionally. I cried out for salvation at age nine, and was baptized in the Holy Spirit at age twelve.

Being constantly involved in Christian ministry as a wounded soldier of Christ and in private psychotherapy since the 70's didn't take the wounded-ness of my past away. In the year 2000 I was declared legally disabled. I was suffering from severe panic/anxiety disorder, major depression, Irritable Bowel Syndrome, eating disorder, Post Traumatic Stress Disorder, and Affective-Histrionic Disorder. The only hope offered to me was lifetime therapy and medication.

By learning how to take my feelings to the Lord and speaking what He tells me I have been freed from all fear caused by my years of abuse. I was healed of all anger, hatred, self-hatred, and fear and it has caused me to love who God created me to be and delight in suffering righteously for His Name's sake. When I close my eyes, I see Jesus carrying me when I can no longer walk. I no longer have open sores of pain. I am in God's healing process. He is with me, past, present, and future. He talks to me through His Holy Spirit and His Word, gives me fellowship with His saints, who are my real family, victory of all sin and the works of Satan, and the quest to share His hope with others along my path of life.

Hidden In Christ,
From a Wounded to a Healed
Soldier of Christ Jesus, My Lord

I will call upon the Lord,
who is worthy to be praised;
So shall I be saved from my

enemies.
The pangs of death surrounded
Me,
And the floods of ungodliness
made me afraid.
The sorrows of Sheol
surrounded me;
The snares of death confronted
Me.
In my distress I called upon the Lord,
And cried out to my God;
He heard my voice from His temple,
And my cry came before Him,
Even to His ears.
Psalm 18:3-6

Hello! I was so anxious to e-mail you both and fill you in on how things have been going. It seems like it has been a long time since I finished going through your ministry because I am living a brand new life. Many of the things I was going through are so far out of reach now that I can barely think on them, let alone feel them. I never in my wildest dreams thought that I could be just a normal person with what are considered normal thoughts, feelings, and reactions. I used to believe that I was going to die without ever knowing how to be happy or experience joy, love, peace, etc. I hated myself so much and I hated just going through the motions of life.

In case you haven't guessed it, things are changing for me. My whole world is changing thanks to the healing power of Jesus Christ! I don't have all of that hatred in my heart anymore—hatred toward myself, my mom, people in my life that have hurt me. It is all completely gone! That is not to say I am glad I lived through the things I lived through, because I am not. I just don't feel ruled by my past any longer. I am beginning to experience a new freedom inside of me that I never thought I would experience. Sometimes I still wish I would have had a different childhood, but that is all it is now—a small wish in the back of my mind. It is not a control or a bunch of bitter, angry, messed up feelings.

My relationship with my husband is better now than it has ever been. He is starting to get to know me, the real me. We are communicating and understanding each other more now. When he touches me, my entire body no longer cringes. I am not to the point where I desire to be, but at least it doesn't make me want to die anymore. I am much more relaxed and at ease sitting by him, holding his hand, hugging, and kissing. I know he notices the difference in me and it makes him happy and he feels like I love him. I know I do love him, but I am still learning about what love is and how to give and receive love.

I will extol You , O Lord,
For You have lifted me up,
And have not let my foes
Rejoice over me.
O Lord my God, I cried out to
You,
And You healed me.
Psalm 30:1, 2

Wow! I don't know where to start. I want you to know that I have had a wonderful week since my return. I have had many occasions to let the enemy in the front door but I have decided that he can have no more entrance in my life. I have had enough of him to last me a lifetime. I had no problem at church when I came back; in fact it went even better than I could have hoped for. I had to turn it all over to Jesus though because I knew I couldn't do what I did with out the help of my Savior. And of course He came through for me just like you said He would.

I have been a Christian for almost nine years and I don't think I ever really believed that Jesus was there for me and lived inside of me. I know now through your help and God's healing power that I have a living Savior that resides in me and helps me through anything that this world tries to throw my way. I can't begin to count all the times I have heard in my head your words; "We brag about our living God but if we don't talk with Him and walk with Him and allow Him in our lives He may as well be dead." That has helped me to remember that my God is a God of promise and He is faithful to His holy word. I really can rely on Him to help me make it through any situation. I am not going to lie and say it has been easy. There have been so many times in the past week that I have had to slap myself awake and remind myself that God is with me and in me and I must allow Him to shine through my actions or those who I have contact with won't know Him like I do.

I have sat and relived my memories in my head and heart just to test myself or maybe I am really testing God to see if He really healed me of those awful things that have haunted me all of my fifty years. I don't mean to test Him but I want to make sure they can't hurt me or my family any more. I am able to replay those things in my head and there is no more pain or hurt or sadness or fear. I am healed and I can be all that God planned for me to be now.

I have so much more that I want to tell you about but for now I will write this just to let you know I am living now, not surviving. Anytime I need help all I do is ask Jesus to take over and show me the problem and we sort it out together. If I can't handle the situation then He takes over and I let Him have it. My God is a God of faithfulness and full of love for me...

God Bless
Love from one who is Victorious

Sing praise to the Lord,
You saints of His,
And give thanks at the
remembrance of His holy
Name.
For His anger is but for a
Moment,
His favor is for life;
Weeping may endure for a
Night,
But joy comes in the morning.
Psalm 30:4, 5

One thing I would like to make clear from the beginning is that I am no different from anyone else born in the fact that we all have an enemy (Satan) who seeks to destroy us as soon as any door of access becomes available to him. I am sure many of you who are reading this book have sadly experienced worse things than I could even imagine. All I have is what I have experienced and my only desire is that my testimony bring glory and honor to all God, Jesus and the Holy Spirit have done in me to bring me to the place where I could *receive* all Jesus died for me to have—PEACE, really does exist.

When I was five years old, my dad went into a violent fit of rage when I spilled my milk at dinner. I remember being passed out a window to a neighbor and hiding in the bushes and the police coming and taking him away. My mom was crying. I don't remember ever seeing him again. In my mind, if I hadn't spilled my milk he wouldn't have gotten upset, we would still be together, and my mom would be happy. I made vows never to do anything to make my mom sad again.

The first time I was molested was when I was seven. The manager of the apartment complex we lived in had kids that I played with. He said he had "something special" to show me. The next day he brought me a football I had always wanted, but I didn't want to take it. My mom said I was being rude and what was wrong with me. I knew if I took the football he was buying my silence. I never did play with that football and kept it for over thirty years.

My mom met a new guy a few years later and was really happy for the first time that I could remember. She told me she wanted to get married and that he wanted to "adopt" me. I guess I was supposed to be excited that he wanted to be my dad but he was already messing with me and all I could think was, "How am I going to survive the next eight years until I can leave home?" A couple of years later we moved closer to his parents and would go visit them on weekends. His dad (my step-grandpa) came to me and said he knew what was going on and he said, "If you want your mom to stay happy you will keep your mouth shut!" From that time on he began to do his thing to me as well (How could he have known the one thing to say to keep my mouth silent?).

The one thing that was especially confusing to me was how we could go to church every Sunday and on weekends when my mom worked he would have me in his bedroom as soon as we got home from church. How can someone say they have Jesus as their Savior and do that? It messed me up for years.

When I was a junior in high school, an evangelist came to our church and preached on Hell so hard I knew I was heading there and I did not want to go there so I asked Jesus to save me. However, for most of my Christian walk I did not know much about the LOVE of God. Oh, I wanted God, wanted to have His perfect will worked in me, but to see Him as my loving Father, which was something to good to be true.

Soon after, I met my husband; he was a Christian and in my naïve thinking Christian guys would be different from all the other boys I'd dated. Wrong, they have the same flesh to deal with and this solidified in me that the only thing I was good for was sex. However, he asked me to marry him so I said yes.

The next ten years I did my best to just be happy, love Jesus and start a family. After our third baby, my step-dad came onto me again. I was in a state of mind where I no longer kept quiet. I told my mom what he had done and also a bit of what had happened growing up. She called me for months asking me if I wanted her to leave him. I refused to tell her what I thought she should do, I couldn't understand her not either leaving him or at the very least getting some kind of counseling. Everything had to be such a secret! Mom was so stressed when I went to get help and even called my friends to see why it was necessary for me to have to go to someone to talk about what had happened. According to her, "I needed to just forgive and get on with my life." Like I hadn't tried that for the last ten years.

The most devastating blow was when I told my husband what my dad had done and he never confronted him about it. I basically, completely shut down and spiraled into severe depression. The only thing that kept me going was my kids. I was able to keep them fed, have them in clean clothes and go to their activities. Everything else fell apart. My housekeeping was a disgrace, I had to pay a counselor to be my friend and felt completely alone in my desire to be healed of the unbearable emotional pain I was in. My husband had no problem with me going to get help as long as he didn't have to be involved in any way. It's not that I expected him to have any answers; however, his support would have been so helpful.

I read everything I could get my hands on in the hopes of being healed. I read every Joyce Meyer book, got in every prayer line so desperately wanting to receive this "peace" Jesus talked about in the Bible. A lady at church said she would help me. She introduced me to the concept that God wanted to be my Father and loved me and was not mad at me. God really taught me a lot about Himself and His love for me using this lady. I grew to trust her like I had never trusted anyone. One of the things that haunted me was that sometimes I had felt pleasure physically during times my step-dad had done things to me. I thought if she didn't reject me after finding out one of my deepest, darkest secrets, then maybe God could forgive me for what a dirty, shameful person I was. After I told her she assured me that your body responds to touch and that is how we were made and that I wasn't evil or dirty. Soon after, things happened in her life where she no longer called me and the devil came in like a flood with rejection and all his lies that were backed up with so many facts and feelings supporting them.

I became a professional "plastic person". I basically just existed for the next couple of years. Deep down somewhere in my spirit man I knew Jesus had died for me to have LIFE. Just existing from day to day certainly was not what He had died on the cross for. I was in the frame of mind where my only chances to experience this "Life" was for Jesus to return or for me to die and then when I got to heaven I would be free of all this emotional pain. Feelings, I completely shut them down, feeling was too dangerous. I ate myself up to over two hundred and sixty pounds, after all Christians can't drink or do drugs, (eating to deaden pain is just as sinful as either of those; it's all a choice of something over God).

Hope deferred makes the heart sick. That Proverb is so true. BUT GOD, one weekend had me in church when this guest speaker talked about how, if we let Jesus speak truth to our pain, we can really be free—HOPE was sparked in me. Could I really live and make my life count for God? Was peace something that could be experienced here on earth not just in heaven? Could I really, really be free and healed from all the emotional torment in my mind? I had to find out. I could not go on one more day like this.

I won't tell you coming out of the prison I was in was easy. Going back to memories that haunt you every waking moment is hell on earth. BUT FREEDOM is REAL! As I was led to ask Jesus what He had to say about me in each of my memories, He was there EVERY time to speak His Words of Truth to me. As I walked through all the painful experiences of my life He also taught me much on forgiveness. Everyone who has ever hurt us has, or is blinded to the effects their actions or words resulted in wounding us. If they truly, truly knew and understood the devastation their actions would bring they would not do them. The times He showed me I needed to forgive but I knew I did not have the strength in me to do it myself, when I asked Him to help me, He did, every time; He was faithful every time. The picture He gave me was that I was like a balloon and all the anger and bitterness went out of me like the air escaping a balloon and then His peace and love replaced all the anger, bitterness, and un-forgiveness.

The greatest thing of all I have come to know and receive is God as my Father and His love for me. The Father I never thought existed or could ever have is REAL. He is a Father who will NEVER, ever hurt me. He is the Father I always wanted, never thought I could have BUT TRULY CAN! Jesus died to restore us to fellowship with the Father. Nobody loves me like Jesus. He left everything to restore you and me to Him. My prayer is that you will let nothing stop you from learning how to "ASK" Jesus to speak His Truth to your pain. James 4:2b says; *"ye desire to have, and can not obtain: ye fight and war, yet ye have not, because ye 'ask' not."* (KJV) One of the lies I believed was it was bad to be needy. This caused me to not set myself up to be let down by anyone ever again. God asked me this question: "Is Jesus powerful?" I answered, "Yes." He then took me to John 5:19, *"The Son can do nothing of himself."* Let Him break you like He did me to come to the place where I know I can do nothing without Him; NOTHING. My every move I must have His strength and grace to do anything, I truly can do NOTHING without Him. To come to the place where He guides and directs my every step is so unbelievably freeing. It is so exhausting to be on guard every second to protect yourself from being hurt. It's not that you won't be hurt ever again, it's just that you come to understand they don't know what they are really doing so it is easy to forgive them and pray for them to not be blinded anymore, and that all the Love that Jesus is becomes real to them.

This is my prayer for you (insert your name in the blanks):

"That Christ may dwell in _______ heart by faith; that ______, being rooted and grounded in love, may be able to comprehend with all saints what is the breadth, and length, and depth, and height; and to know the love of Christ, which passes all knowledge, that ____ might be filled with all the fullness of God. Amen."

Blessings to you all.

I will extol You, O Lord,
For You have lifted me up,
And have not let my foes
Rejoice over me.
O Lord my God, I cried out to
You,
And You healed me,
(Psalm 30:1, 2)

I thank God that He is able to lead me into triumph as I allow Him to be in charge of my life's situations.

I grew up in a divorced home and lacked in receiving affirmation. The absence of good can be just as damaging as the presence of evil. It was very hard for me to speak, to have a voice, and I seemed fearful when having to share my feelings with anyone about anything.

In school I would always opt for an "F" if my lessons had anything to do with standing in front of the classroom. I spent endless time preparing for book reports, poems and all sorts of projects, but there was no way I could stand in front of the classroom and speak. The one thing I really wanted to be in school was a cheerleader, probably because my big sister was one. I remember the day of tryouts. Man, could I jump and do all the moves, but I was a cheerleader without a voice. The two just don't mix! I was so horribly disappointed in myself because I was unable to be and do the things that interested me the most.

No adults in my life seemed to be there to help me pull myself out of my shell while growing up. I'm sure it was nice to have someone quiet since I came from a family of eight children, so coping became a great part of my life. "This is the way life is and you can't change it," became very familiar to me in my thinking. During my upbringing there was a saying that "children should be seen and not heard," and I can tell you from personal experience that it became an intimidator of my soul; making me feel of no value or purpose. I had no voice and inside I wanted so much for someone to know what was going on inside of me.

My mother left our home when I was five years of age and my dad took it upon himself to keep all of my sisters and brothers under one roof; for which I will always be thankful. My dad remarried by the time I was eight and he was busy with his new life and part of the old life of drinking and gambling. As my sisters and brothers graduated and left home, I really had no one to communicate with. I had a few close friends growing up. I was very introverted and I realize now that it is partly due to my melancholy temperament, but also the environment in which I was raised added to my fear of rejection and fear of, "What if I'm wrong."

As I became an adult, my shyness continued to keep me from trying to experience new things. My husband became my prince and he even became my voice. He would protect me by answering for me and I really appreciated it. He was kind, caring, and was such an encouragement. He could see value in me and helped me overcome many fears. This may sound stupid to you as the reader, but I hated to talk on the phone if anyone was in the room. I hated and refused to deal with any form of confrontation and my husband graciously helped me and taught me how to deal with confrontation and how important it was for me to confront rather than hide behind the walls of fear.

When I accepted Christ as my Savoir I began to hear things about all the potential that was in me, and it was fearful because I didn't see in my carnal mind how I could possibly accomplish anything. I was taught to find scripture and use it to help me overcome my fear. 2Timothy 1:7 was my daily prayer, "*God didn't give me a spirit of fear, but of love, power and a sound mind.*" It really helped my confidence and I began to draw on God to give me strength. With inner strength from God, I was beginning to talk more and at times didn't want my husband to answer for me. I began to realize I did have value and I did have a voice. My husband was the first person who helped me get out from behind the many walls I was hiding behind because he helped me see who I was in Christ.

Five years ago, I was asked to minister in a women's conference and I was very hesitant, but I agreed to be a part of the conference. The closer it came, the fear began to haunt me. My mind was telling me all sorts of negative input and I was quoting 2Timothy 1:7 each day to overcome the fear. A few days before the conference, I just felt like I would not be able to minister in front of these ladies. I had decided to call the leader and tell her not to count on me. I was devastated and felt not only fear was holding me back, but that I was a complete failure because I couldn't keep my word.

I knew I needed some quiet time with God, so I put on worship music and began telling God the fear was too overwhelming. I even asked Him why I was so afraid; it was beyond normal fear, more like terror. I would find myself holding my breath, praying it would go away. As I was praying, the Lord showed me a memory of me around the age of nine years old. My sister and her husband, who had just come home from the armed services, asked if I would come and live with them. My dad and step mom agreed and so I went off to another town to live with them.

A week or so had passed by and in this memory; the Lord was showing me at the kitchen table with my brother-in-law. I knew that my sister was not there and I watched closely as to what was going on. My brother-in-law was putting a shell in his revolver. I saw him put only one bullet in, he then spun the chamber, put the gun to his head and asked if I had ever played Russian roulette. Of course, I had no clue what that was, but I knew this was a game I didn't want to be a part of. My heart was beginning to pulsate rapidly as he put the gun to his head and told me he would pull the trigger and if he didn't die, it would then be my turn to put the gun to my head and pull the trigger. I know I quit breathing at that very second and ran as fast as I could go to get out of the house. My problem was since I had only been there a week, I really didn't know the neighbors nor had friends to go to, and so I ran across the street and beat on the neighbor's door with all my might. No one came to the door, so I rushed right in the house and ran into the living room where I found a big over-stuffed chair to hide behind. I wasn't sure if I was being followed and I dared not look for fear that I was being chased. Then what would I do?!

As I sat behind the chair, my heart was pounding. It was the only thing I could actually hear in this stranger's house. I was petrified I would be found and I held my breath and was totally in a frozen position so no one could hear me.

I don't know how much time passed, but I was awakened by a knock on the kitchen door and I could hear my sister ask the lady if she had seen me. The woman replied to her and said she hadn't. It was such a great relief to hear my sister's voice and I scrambled from behind the chair to the kitchen door in a flash. The woman was quite surprised I was in her house and my sister took me home. Immediately, I was taken back to my father's house. No one spoke of the event and I had never told anyone about this incident until the Lord brought this to my attention. I somehow knew in my heart that my brother-in-law truly didn't want me to be a part of his family and I had no voice to tell my story.

The Lord at that moment showed me how the spirit of fear had overcome me. The lie was that I was all alone, no one to protect me and that I was going to die. I asked Him why He hadn't helped me and He spoke to my spirit and said that He was there with me and He protected me during that time. I was overcome with peace and it reminded me of the scripture that says, "I will never, never, never leave you or forsake you." Amp.

These are what everyone calls those "deep, dark secrets," and these secrets are what keeps Christians and non-Christians alike from finding perfect peace, until Peace himself comes in and gives you truth.

I was able to speak at the women's conference that weekend because fear had been erased with God's truth. Peace was with me and I thank God for His loving kindness to help me overcome this breathtaking fear that immobilized me so many times in life situations.

I can always call on God for inner strength and I know He will grace me for that time of need. I thank God for the word, for Jesus is the Word. I am also a believer in the fact that the Holy Spirit's desire is for us to be healed not only spiritually and physically but also emotionally and He is the only True One who knows how to get us to that point of freedom. He not only renewed my mind by His word, but through experience He took me to my place of pain and spoke truth into my soul. Whether the truth be written or spoken, both are directed by the unction of the Holy Ghost; and the result is that the truth will make you free.

I have had experience with the Holy Spirit showing me where I needed to forgive my mother; this was a year after she had passed away. I had always made excuses of why she did what she did. The Lord showed me that my reasoning was a way to cope with my pain and that I had to admit she really hurt me emotionally. After I forgave her from the heart, I felt so released and was able to cry. I realized I wouldn't let her hurt me again and had made up my mind I wouldn't cry at her funeral and had never really grieved her passing away. The Lord truly carried my sorrow and grief that day. After that healing, I recognized that I had compassion on others rather than feel like they just needed to deal with their pain as I had done for years. This is a good sign of freedom; when your actions begin to produce good fruit. We need freedom ourselves to help others in their pain.

This is the reason I have a testimony to share with others, so that they may find hope in Jesus Christ, Who is the Hope of Glory.

I sought the Lord, and He
Heard me,
and delivered me from all my fears.
They looked to Him and were radiant,
And their faces were not ashamed.
This poor man cried out,
And the Lord heard him,
and saved him out of all his troubles.
(Psalm 34:4 – 6)

Appendix V

Welcome to the Family of God

If you just prayed to receive Jesus for the first time, I would appreciate it if you would let me know so we can be praying for you. You may contact us through the following Web sites:

www.GenuineChristianity.org
www.GenuineChristian.org.

This is the most important decision you have ever or ever will make. You need to fully understand what you have done or are doing. This is not just an end-of-life insurance policy. This is the beginning of LIFE for you and potentially your family as well.

There is no such thing as a stupid question so ask what is on your heart. For instance, if you were expecting to feel something after you asked Jesus to come in and didn't, don't worry about it, just let me know. If you felt something and it frightened you let me know that as well. It is my desire to help you get settled in the family of God.

To help you learn, we have created the Genuine Christianity Study Guide. Check our website,

www.GenuineChristianity.org or www.GenuineChristian.org, for the current availability of the *Genuine Christianity Study Guide.*

Welcome Home friend!

Bibliography

New King James Version of the Holy Bible. Copyright ©1979, 1980, 1982 Thomas Nelson, Inc.

The New Testament Modern English Revised Standard Edition, J. B. Phillips. Copyright ©J. B. Phillips, 1958, 1959, 1960, 1972. Published by Macmillan Publishing Company, 866 Third Avenue, New York, NY 10022.

The Amplified Bible. Copyright ©1962, 1964, 1965, 1977, 1986 Zondervan Corporation.

The Amplified New Testament. Copyright ©1958, 1987.

The Amplified Gospel of John. Copyright ©1954, 1987 Lockman Foundation, La Habra, CA 90631.

The Message — The Bible in Contemporary Language, Eugene H. Peterson. Copyright © 1993, 1994, 1995, 1996, 2000, 2001, 2002. Used by permission of NavPress Publishing

Group. NavPress P.O. Box 35001 Colorado Springs, CO 80935.

The Hebrew-Greek Key Study Bible, Authorized King James Version, Zodhiates' original and complete system of Bible study. Compiled and edited by Spiros Zodhiates, Th.D. Copyright ©1984 by Spiros Zodhiates and AMG International, Inc., D/B/A AMG Publishers, Chattanooga, TN 37422.

Holy Bible, New International Version®. NIV®. Copyright ©1973, 1978, 1984 by International Bible Society, used by permission of Zondervan Publishing House. All rights reserved.

NIV and *New International Version* are trademarks registered in the United States Patent and Trademark Office by the International Bible Society. Use of either trademark requires the permission of the International Bible Society.

Competent to Counsel, Dr. Jay E. Adams. Copyright ©1970 by Jay E. Adams, published by Presbyterian and Reformed Publishing Company, Phillipsburg, New Jersey 08865, p. xviii, p. 1, 2.

General Index

A true revelation from God, 222
abandonment, 82
abide in Him, 9, 103, 108
abiding in Christ, 10, 107
abreaction, 62
abstinence, 89
active listening, 15
addictive, 82
affirmation, 82, 277
agape, 8, 95, 98
aletheia, 59
alter, 87, 239, 240
Amplified, 11, 99, 220
Anger management, 233
apathy, 76, 83, 116, 147, 201, 229
Apathy, 229
arguments, 115, 116, 117, 119
armor, 126, 127, 129
authority, 24, 31, 38, 124, 125, 126, 127, 128, 129, 130, 161,

165, 167, 179, 232
bad feelings, 16, 56, 66, 71, 72, 85, 105, 144, 178, 228, 229, 230, 231, 237
behavior, 60, 66, 82, 83, 84, 91, 92, 96, 170, 176, 178, 223, 240, 241, 256, 257, 258
blame game, 73, 105
born again, 7, 10, 19, 20, 21, 23, 24, 25, 27, 60, 69, 82, 108
born again experience, 20
brokenhearted, 10, 67, 208, 209, 258
cares, 40, 68, 75, 88, 106, 144, 153, 226, 227, 228, 231, 237
Christ like, 20, 107
Christian confession, 195
cognitive, 49, 54, 57, 75, 101, 118, 243
commitment, 6
communication, 5, 13, 14, 16, 17, 48, 57, 59, 65, 68, 72, 85, 101, 117, 128, 133, 214, 248, 250
Competent to Counsel, 55, 74
compulsive, 82, 208
confidence in God, 12, 55, 68, 197, 237, 258
cope, 39, 68, 208, 230, 282
cope-able, 75
coping mechanism, 74, 75, 105, 176, 256
coping mechanisms, 73, 116, 229
Counselor, 24, 179, 195, 206
cross, 2, 8, 10, 60, 80, 93, 100, 103, 127, 128, 161, 181, 274
demonic activity, 133
Denial, 68
depression, 120, 200, 201, 206, 207, 210, 273
Divine order, 146, 248
divine protection, 24
Divorce, 135
drug usage, 75

Emotion, 54
emotional need, 82
emotional pain, 10, 3, 16, 51, 54, 60, 70, 72, 74, 85, 88, 89, 105, 133, 152, 175, 209, 230, 235, 243, 255, 256, 274, 275
emotional reflexes, 57
emotional wound, 82, 83
empty tomb, 36
end-of-life insurance policy, 283
endurance, 33, 72
entolē, 106, 177
eternal life, 22, 27
experience the truth, 55
experiential, 48, 49, 54, 55, 56, 57, 58, 60, 118
experiential condition, 57, 58
experiential memory, 48, 49, 54, 55, 56, 60, 118
experts, 194, 209
faith, 5, 6, 7, 11, 17, 20, 22, 23, 24, 26, 27, 28, 32, 33, 35, 37, 43, 45, 47, 48, 49, 50, 51, 55, 66, 68, 70, 72, 77, 80, 86, 96, 106, 110, 117, 127, 128, 129, 132, 155, 165, 179, 187, 188, 190, 201, 218, 221, 226, 227, 228, 229, 231, 236, 237, 246, 247, 249, 250, 261, 276
false beliefs, 48, 49, 53, 66
family of God, 23
Family of God, 283
feminine side, 71
free, 8, 3, 5, 6, 9, 25, 26, 29, 31, 53, 54, 59, 60, 68, 73, 82, 85, 88, 89, 90, 92, 104, 116, 132, 134, 135, 158, 166, 207, 213, 234, 236, 242, 249, 250, 253, 258, 259, 266, 275, 282
garments of white, 64
generic prayer, 227
gentle knowing, 15, 62, 84
ginosko, 59

God is alive, 35
God's will, 4, 53
gold, 47, 62, 80, 238
great harvest, 6, 7
grief, 70, 71, 101, 183, 282
growing spiritually, 36
halo, 205
hardens your heart, 68
holiness, 79, 205
holy, 11, 28, 31, 79, 80, 81, 83, 87, 88, 93, 104, 145, 157, 178, 253, 261, 270, 271
Holy Bible, 11, 19, 28, 29, 30, 31, 33, 91
holy life, 79, 80, 81, 93
holy living, 83
Holy Spirit, 2, 7, 10, 11, 12, 20, 28, 31, 32, 33, 56, 59, 66, 67, 72, 100, 101, 102, 105, 108, 111, 120, 121, 125, 140, 143, 147, 162, 167, 175, 180, 195, 196, 200, 206, 209, 213, 243, 253, 267, 271, 281, 282
homosexuals, 89
horizontal, 13, 17, 102, 221
horizontal relationship, 8
I'm only human, 24, 176
inadequate, 11, 151, 218, 235
incarnated, 20, 176
incorruptible seed, 27
inner pain, 5, 9, 51, 58, 69, 70, 73, 77, 100, 109, 195
inner peace, 11, 12, 37, 45, 51, 76, 91, 106, 119, 140, 144, 180, 200, 211, 262
inner turmoil, 11, 6, 37, 73, 75, 89, 124, 177, 179, 205, 228, 262
intellect, 48, 54
Intellectual love, 96
Interpretation, 54

intimate, 48
kainos, 97
kingdom of darkness, 125
Kingdom of Light, 125, 126
lies, 31, 48, 49, 51, 54, 57, 59, 60, 65, 66, 69, 70, 73, 87, 88, 93, 100, 101, 107, 129, 133, 176, 210, 211, 229, 230, 240, 265, 274, 276
life cycle, 248
listen, 14, 27, 84, 106, 107, 108, 119, 121, 125, 159, 191, 242
listening. *See* listen
living sacrifice, 87
living without sin, 254
maintenance programs, 76
malcontent, 203, 204
mask, 11, 75, 80
masks of protection, 9
maturation, 48
mature, 8, 26, 48, 49, 79, 80, 87, 101, 105, 110, 133, 186, 212, 223, 237, 253
maturity, 4, 36, 48, 51, 55, 80, 101, 117, 120, 143, 150, 214, 237, 244, 258
medication regiments, 76
meditating, 33
mental transference, 75
Message Translation, 99, 213, 226
mind of Christ, 24
mind renewal, 53, 87
minister restoration, 9
ministers of restoration, 209
misinterpretation, 48, 85
misinterpreted, 54, 85, 86, 101, 106
mission, 1, 2, 125

mood altering drugs, 36, 74, 208
mood-altering drug, 75
mortal human, 24, 177
multitasking, 114
New Testament, 28, 32, 33, 178
NIV, 99
non-legal drugs, 75
obedience, 8, 12, 50, 99, 102, 115, 118, 210
obsessed, 85
Old Testament, 28, 33, 97
only human, 24, 176
pain transference, 76
perfect, 11, 5, 13, 15, 26, 37, 48, 49, 51, 53, 66, 69, 76, 77, 92, 102, 109, 110, 124, 129, 133, 140, 143, 144, 147, 149, 160, 161, 162, 175, 177, 206, 211, 214, 231, 237, 250, 253, 254, 273, 281
permanent freedom, 12, 255
perpetrators, 65
personal Helper, 24
Phillips Translation, 24, 100, 180
Phillips Tsranslation, 82
physical transference, 75
Picture, 54
pornography, 80, 81
Power Plant of life, 201, 203
presentation, 79, 258
problem, promise, process, 4
promise, 4, 29, 37, 50, 51, 56, 76, 92, 178, 187, 188, 257, 270
promises, 49, 73, 178, 180, 237, 247
proper communication, 13
protect, 63, 72, 77, 104, 109, 110, 114, 129, 132, 134, 162, 163, 229, 231, 262, 276, 278, 281

psuchē, 101
Psychology, 74, 76
Psychotherapy, 74
pull you through, 51
purification of our soul, 49
qualitatively new, 97
R&R Ministry Training, 259
rage, 42, 131, 132, 170, 232, 233, 234, 235, 236, 242, 243, 256, 257, 258, 272
regeneration, 56
relate horizontally, 8
relationship, 5, 8, 9, 11, 13, 14, 15, 16, 17, 20, 27, 31, 37, 50, 56, 102, 104, 105, 108, 120, 178, 195, 197, 202, 210, 221, 247, 248, 269
relationship revelation, 11
relevance, 7
religion, 2, 4, 7, 8, 9, 18, 30, 35, 180, 197
religious. *See* religion
renew your mind, 4, 51
renewing of the mind, 49, 229
responding, 3, 15, 17, 57, 66, 255
rest, 22, 25, 41, 42, 66, 67, 73, 75, 76, 77, 81, 102, 104, 105, 106, 108, 124, 136, 181, 195, 213, 214, 220, 237
right brain thinking', 71
sanctification, 55, 56, 229, 237
sanctified by Truth, 55
saving of our soul, 49
secret things, 71
self-defeating works, 9, 258
self-loathing, 60, 64
seminars, 259
sex abusers, 81

sin nature, 20, 69, 254
sin-conscious, 254
sorrow, 70, 71, 249, 282
soul surgery, 88
speak audibly, 22, 118, 159, 245
Speak to the Lord, 117
speaking engagements, 259
Spirit of Truth, 33
spiritual apathy, 2, 116
spiritual death, 76, 116
spiritual growth, 76
stinking thinking, 53
storms of life, 36, 37, 254
stronghold, 115
struggles of life, 47, 48, 214
success, 8, 51, 74, 218
Sunday school picnic, 125, 126
Teacher, 24
throne of grace, 76, 88, 196
torturers, 133, 135, 139
transformation, 53, 229, 236, 237
transformed, 49, 53, 60
transparent, 79
tree of life, 25
trials of life, 48, 49, 51, 79, 101
trust, 27, 43, 44, 47, 48, 49, 50, 51, 66, 68, 88, 106, 110, 121, 137, 152, 186, 188, 189, 219, 237, 266, 274
truth, 16, 17, 18, 29, 31, 51, 53, 54, 56, 59, 60, 62, 63, 64, 66, 68, 69, 71, 72, 80, 82, 85, 88, 90, 91, 93, 95, 99, 100, 101, 103, 106, 107, 126, 129, 146, 167, 168, 169, 174, 175, 178, 210, 217, 221, 222, 223, 229, 231, 236, 254, 265, 275, 281
unresolved anger, 133

vertical, 13, 15, 17, 103, 221
vertical relationship, 8
victory, 116, 117, 121, 123, 127, 129, 153, 219, 220, 267
vision, 1, 2, 146, 150, 151, 201
voice of God, 41, 44, 121, 243
white garments, 62
will of the Lord. *See* God's will
wisdom of heaven, 24, 247
witchcraft, 75
workaholic, 84, 203, 236
WWJD, 181
yoke, 73
zōē type of life, 73

About the Author

After a dramatic encounter with Jesus Christ in 1982, Brother Low began preaching the Gospel and serving the Lord with signs and miracles following.

Immediately following his encounter with Jesus, the Holy Spirit enrolled him in His schooling. For several years, the Holy Spirit would get him up at 4:00 a.m. and teach him the word of God until 6:00 a.m. That personalized training and the necessary, faithful communication with the Holy Spirit helped him understand that Jesus wants a personal, intimate relationship with his children. He also knew from the very beginning that he was called to serve the Lord full time. However, it took nine years before full-time ministry replaced his career in the computer industry.

From the very beginning of his walk with God, his passion has been to know Jesus Christ personally. He has wanted nothing else or less since that day he met Jesus and the Holy Spirit. Since that encounter in 1982, Brother Low has personally witnessed the results of immediately obeying the voice of the Holy Spirit. During many times of his ministry the Lord has raised the physically dead, performed countless physical miracle healings, and set hundreds free from their broken hearts and mental torments. In addition to serving as pastor since 1984, he has been blessed to travel and minister in pastor's conventions and to local churches throughout the United States, Philippines, Haiti, Mexico, and South East Asia. He continues to travel and minister as doors open to him.

Brother Low is the founder and current president of ZOE Ministries and Master's Touch. He continues calling people out of spiritual apathy by teaching the Body how easy it is to hear the voice of God and how quickly Jesus responds to their concerns and fears. His goal is to help the Body step up to a higher walk with God through a lifestyle of Genuine Christianity. His prayer is that church leaders begin to recognize the pain that surrounds them as opportunities awaiting them and their churches.

My greatest joy in ministry is to see the spiritually lifeless come alive in Christ as they personally experience how easy it is to gain His inner peace in their life. When spiritually lifeless persons experience the joy of abiding IN Christ for the first time, revival starts. Nothing is better than that.